Facing Terrorism

Facing Terrorism

Responding as Christians

Edward LeRoy Long Jr.

Westminster John Knox Press
LOUISVILLE • LONDON

Book design by Sharon Adams
Cover design by Jennifer K. Cox
Cover photograph by Paul Chesley/National Geographic Image Collection

First edition
Published by Westminster John Knox Press
Louisville, Kentucky

04 05 06 07 08 09 10 11 12 13 — 10 9 8 7 6 5 4 3 2

Library of Congress Cataloging-in-Publication Data

Long, Edward LeRoy.
    Facing terrorism : responding as Christians / Edward LeRoy Long, Jr.
        p. cm.
    Includes bibliographical references.
    ISBN 0-664-22760-0 (alk. paper)
    1. September 11 Terrorist Attacks, 2001—Religious aspects—
Christianity.   2. Terrorism—Religious aspects—Christianity.   I. Title.

BT736.15.L66 2004
261.8"—dc22   2003064509

Contents

Preface

This book has been written from a realization that terrorism is a form of violence that differs from warfare to an extent and in ways that require a reconsideration and probable modification of the moral categories that Christians have used to think about the use of violence for political purposes and strategies for curtailing or overcoming such violence. Terrorism is not new, but it has recently become more prevalent and the problems it poses more urgent. The events of September 11, 2001, were sufficiently momentous to make it impossible for Americans to ignore this form of violence and unwise to consider the issues it raises as already understandable with the terms historically used for moral thinking about armed conflict between sovereign states.

Christian attitudes toward war have never come to a consensus despite long and extensive attention given to war as a moral problem by scholars over many centuries. The positions that characterize Christian thinking about war are briefly examined in my book *War and Conscience in America,* published in 1968. That book was written to provide an easily accessible description of the alternative views present within the Christian community and to indicate how those differing views were relevant during a conflict that deeply divided both church and nation as to its legitimacy. In that

conflict the various moral judgments were readily identifi-
able and generally understandable even though the differences between them were never resolved.

Points of view about the moral issues raised by terrorism
and by efforts to combat it are not yet sorted out into such
recognizable patterns. People are feeling their way, with the
result that the present discussions of terrorism and the moral
issues that it poses do not have the same contours or the same
consistency as did the discussion of the morality of warfare
in the 1960s. Instead of recognizable disagreements we now
confront diffusion and uncertainty, especially when the categories used to think about the morality of warfare are adopted
to thinking about terrorism without attention to the differences between the problems they address. This means that
the discussion offered here is less a report on a settled pattern
of alternative views than an effort to anticipate where serious
considerations of this issue may eventually lead. I dare say
that this does not make the undertaking any less valuable and
even makes it more important as an effort to facilitate further
reflections and discussion.

In dealing with war as a moral problem, major attention
focuses on whether or not and under what conditions it is
morally legitimate to utilize arms in order to repel aggressive
or threatening behavior. Almost all war involves conflict
between nation-states acting officially. But terrorism is more
complex, and hence broader issues must be examined. It is
necessary to explore the nature and causes of terrorism since
it can be carried out by both nation-states and also—as is
more often the case—by small groups acting without official
warrant. Terrorism will not necessarily be stopped by defeat-
ing it on some field of battle and obtaining an explicit surrender. It will be eliminated only by creating conditions and
expectations in the world that overcome the impulses that
give rise to such behavior. Moreover, facing terrorism
involves not merely looking at the moral standing of efforts

to defeat it but the development of attitudes that will help to mitigate its causes and to sustain a spiritually engendered poise in face of its threats. Dealing with war as a moral problem is one thing; dealing with terrorism as a threatening experience is another.

I have written this book simultaneously with my membership on a task force created by the Presbyterian Church in the United States of America to study the issues posed by terrorism and religiously motivated violence. The work of that task force has provided the impulse to develop this analysis as my own effort to sort out the issues. I want to acknowledge benefits gained from interaction with that group, commend its faithfulness to its charge, express my gratitude for encouraging me to develop this treatment as an individual undertaking, and exonerate it of any endorsement of the views to which I have come before its thinking was finished and its conclusions reached. The report of that group, which will be made after this book is released for publication, will further the inquiry and advance the process this volume tackles in an early and preliminary way.

I have benefitted from critical comments made about drafts of this manuscript as it has developed. The Reverend Robert F. Smylie, who for years headed the Presbyterian Office at the United Nations and whose familiarity with international affairs is outstanding, provided a meticulous examination of an early draft. He saved me from several goofs and provided me with many pertinent additions. Even though I did not take every suggestion he gave me and hence remain personally responsible for what remains in the text, I offer this book as a way of celebrating our scholarly collegiality and honoring his distinctive contribution to the work of the Presbyterian Church (U.S.A.) in the area of peacemaking. I am also indebted to Gary D. Payton, whose long experience in the armed forces and later work with peacemaking has left him with a balanced outlook on both. He offered specific comments that saved me from making some statements that were either inaccurate or pejorative.

Other individuals have offered encouragement and support in a variety of ways, from simple affirmation of the importance of this effort to assistance with specific details about which I have not been certain. I could name a legion, but would leave out somebody who should be mentioned. Many of these individuals are active in shaping the social witness and peacemaking efforts of the Presbyterian Church— giving of their time and talent to thinking how the moral mandates of the gospel call for active involvement with the affairs of the world and for diligent inquiry into matters like those that are addressed in this book. Working with them under the able staff leadership supporting this process has been one of the deep satisfactions of my career as a scholar.

May we as Christians encourage all just and thoughtful efforts to deal with terrorism, both by those who bear political responsibilities in a global world and by those who work from commitments to various philanthropic and religious communities, and may we lend our support to the fashioning of a world order in which fairness has eliminated injustice, compassion supplanted hate, freedom overcome oppression, and modesty replaced truculence.

Edward LeRoy Long Jr.
Providence Point
Pentecost 2003

Chapter 1

What Is Terrorism?

*I*t is important to have a clear idea of what we mean by terrorism in order to cope with the particular and peculiar dangers it poses, but defining terrorism proves to be a difficult task. The term has been employed in many ways to designate a whole range of activities that make people feel threatened. The result is that the term refers to many things that people dislike just as "motherhood" refers to many things people like. Because this happens, violence that is not intended as terrorism is often tarred with a designation that serves more to express disapproval than to point out a special kind of action. The features that characterize terrorism are lost in a cloud of rhetorical confusion. As one writer puts it:

> The concern about definitions, besides reflecting any scholar's commendable interest in being precise about one's subject matter, stems from the damage done by the countless twisted and polemical uses through the years of the term "terrorism." The one thing on which every user of the term agrees is that terrorism is bad. So it has been a catch-all pejorative, applied mainly to matters involving force or political authority in some way but sometimes applied even more broadly to just about any disliked action associated with someone else's policy agenda.[1]

1

Terrorism is behavior that uses violence or the threat to use violence to create fear in order to further some purpose, if only the purpose of venting anger against that which its perpetrators dislike. It is not the only form of behavior that seeks to frighten its opponents, but it is a particularly threatening form of such behavior because of its stealth, unpredictability, and potential for avoiding direct responsibility for its actions. Consequently, it differs from the uses of violence that have traditionally been considered appropriate ways to achieve political purposes that cannot be achieved by so-called peaceful means. Terrorism may frighten people even more than aggressive warfare because, although like such warfare it attacks them, it does not take the form of planned and organized campaigns openly conducted. Terrorism frightens people even more than accidents do because, although like accidents it occurs without predictability, unlike accidents it is driven by anger or malice.

Perhaps the best way to approach the concept of terrorism is to start with a definition from the public sphere. The United States government uses the following description to indicate the activities it monitors as instances of terrorist activity. Terrorism is "premeditated, politically motivated violence perpetrated against noncombatant targets by subnational groups or clandestine agents, usually intended to influence an audience."[2] This definition excludes actions that are committed in momentary surges of blind rage—instances of which might well create a great deal of fear but do not represent an ongoing political threat. It also excludes actions done by individuals for personal gain or out of personal hate—actions that would be more appropriately called crimes. This definition indicates that the targets must be noncombatants—that is, persons who are not equipped with the necessary means of protecting themselves against attack. This would normally designate civilians but it could also designate members of military units when off duty. Finally, terrorist activities are designed to be seen by others, not only to be felt by the victims.[3]

But despite the distinguishing features enumerated in the foregoing definition, there are a number of antinomies that mark the way in which people have tried to understand terrorism. These antinomies show up as strong contrasts between two ways of looking at terrorism, each of which is warranted but may leave out contrasting considerations. These antinomies illumine the difficulties in describing terrorism and may well suggest that no single view of its nature is adequate.

Deliberate Strategy or Impulsive Drive?

One of the questions that occurs in the discussion of terrorism is whether it is a form of political action or whether it develops out of some psychological conditions that prompt the use of violence in a wanton manner. The rubrics "deliberate strategy" and "impulsive drive" describe the two views that constitute the first antinomy; they are not overly judgmental. The first view considers terrorism to be a form of political action. The second view considers it an outgrowth of a psychic drive. In a major study of the origins of terrorism published in 1998, these two views are juxtaposed. An initial chapter develops the first idea; a second chapter, the second. Under the rubric of deliberate strategy, terrorism is viewed as "a willful choice made by an organization for political and strategic reasons, rather than the unintended outcome of psychological or social factors."[4] The contrasting way of looking at terrorism "argues that *political terrorists are driven to commit acts of violence as a consequence of psychological forces,* and that their special psycho-logic is constructed to rationalize *acts they are psychologically compelled to commit.*"[5] Although, as both of these authors and the editor of the book acknowledge, these two ways of understanding terrorism may not be mutually exclusive, nevertheless an understanding of terrorism coming from one perspective emphasizes features that differ from an understanding of terrorism coming from the other perspective.

To look at terrorism as a strategy is to assume that terrorists make a rational decision to seek some change in the policies or the behavior of groups they consider enemies. The consequence (or consequences) they seek may be to change the behavior of some political entity whose policies they consider unacceptable. Compared to other ways of seeking political change, terrorism is remarkably inexpensive. A few plane tickets and a few handguns obtained to carry out a highly visible calamity can be used with shrewd planning and ruthless resolve to create as much clout as might be achieved by military means supported by budgets in the billions. The seizure of even a few hostages can put governments with enormous resources and supposedly impressive strength into uncomfortable quandaries, as those governments have to weigh the moral duty to protect the innocent lives of those who have been captured against the obligation to adhere to their own plans and purposes and not succumb to the threat posed by the terrorists.

Terrorism as strategy would be open to examination on a cost-benefit analysis, even if that terminology is not generally used by terrorists. Although financially inexpensive, other "costs" can be very high. The use of violence without the official sanction of a sovereign state is likely to create a backlash that will push the public (particularly those whose well-being is adversely affected) to a very high level of anger. Terrorist actions committed to gain support for a cause may indeed create opposition to it. People may be somewhat accustomed to accept the use of armed forces by a nation as a part of statecraft, but they are likely to view violence from rogue groups as entirely illegitimate. The demand for retribution that may result can be extremely strong and perhaps even vindictive. This means that terrorists may lose whatever potential sympathy exists for their cause, not only from those who are attacked but from others as well. Terrorism creates fear, and fear quickly can translate into an intense level of anger that becomes especially vehement and resolute. Attacks made upon military installations by the armed forces of a hostile country using ordinary weapons are troubling enough and will usually bring military counteraction (as Pearl Harbor demonstrated), but attacks made upon civilian targets by unidentified persons using means that are ordinarily associated with peaceful activities (such as passenger planes) are infuriating and may create a very strong impulse for punitive action (as the attacks on the World Trade Center and the Pentagon show). Pearl Harbor brought the United States into a war that was already going on; the attacks of September 11 created an even more extensive resolve to combat terrorism in broad and perhaps as yet undetermined ways, even to wage a war that would not have garnered public support before the event took place.

What, then, other than the minimization of monetary outlay, might be reasons why terrorism is employed for strategic purposes? There is a sense in which terrorism allows groups that otherwise have no access to power to make their wishes known and agendas felt. It can undercut the ease with which rich and powerful nations exercise control over all aspects of international life and thus seem to have their way almost unchallenged. Terrorism enables the disinherited to bring their dissatisfactions to the fore, making it impossible to ignore them or keep from having to deal with their concerns as a problem. Terrorism, writes Martha Crenshaw, "inspires resistance by example. As propaganda of the deed, terrorism demonstrates that the regime can be challenged, and that illegal opposition is possible. It acts as a catalyst, not a substitute for mass revolt. All the tedious and time-consuming organizational work of mobilizing the people can be avoided."[6] To be sure, strong nations are threatened by this and therefore may react against it with intensified vehemence. But that reaction may even be something that the terrorists like to see happen. For instance, countries that cherish freedom will often, as chapter 4 will point out, tend to curtail their own liberties in order to make themselves more secure. This can be something that some terrorists or their associates may consider to be worth achieving. Moreover, terrorists can with very little monetary outlay and perhaps with even a relatively limited amount of risk place nations in the position of having to respond with massive resources to counter the threat. No other kind of violence offers such economical effectiveness. It is little wonder that strong nations which pride themselves on the efficacy of their massive systems of defense are upset by this. The result is a bit like terrorist Davids challenging superpower Goliaths.

The choice of terrorism as a means to achieve some political objective is "often the last in a sequence of choices."[7] In this respect, terrorism when understood as a strategy makes the same appeal as does just-war thinking, namely, that violence is employed only as a last resort. This is something of a moral judgment—involving the premise that all other (supposedly preferable) methods have been tried and proven unsuccessful. All claims to have exhausted other remedies are, of course, debatable, since the decision about whether or not all alternatives have been tried and found wanting is made by those who seek to legitimize their own resort to violence. As is frequently the case with those who take up arms in an allegedly just cause, claims made by terrorists to have exhausted all other means are usually advanced as rationalizations for chosen actions. Such claims seldom, if ever, come as a result of adjudication by impartial observers in a way that gives them independent credibility.

But rather than being understood as a strategy, terrorism can also be considered an outgrow of a psychic malfeasance. Terrorists often vent anger against those whose power or whose practices are perceived by them as threatening. This alternative way of looking at terrorism stresses its roots in attitudes and feelings—of hostility, deprivation, and resentment. Instead of being strategic, terrorism as understood in this way is

> polarizing and absolutist, it is a rhetoric of "us versus them," it is a rhetoric without nuance, without shades of gray. "They," the establishment, are the cause of all evil, in vivid contrast to "us," the freedom fighters, consumed by righteous rage. And if "they" are the sources of our problems, it follows ineluctably, in the special psycho-logic of the terrorist, that "they" must be destroyed. It is the only just and moral thing to do. Once the basic premises are accepted, the logical reasoning is flawless.[8]

Many of us would probably use the term "pathological" to describe those who engage in terrorism for psychological reasons. But Jerold M. Post, the author of the chapter from which this quotation is taken, prefers to see the actions of terrorists as springing more from a particular psycho-logic rather than from a frame of mind that can be considered sick. That judgment is based on the realization that many terrorists are extremely astute and able to undertake their operations in ways that exhibit considerable rational acumen. Yet, although he refrains from using the pejorative term "pathological," this same author argues that the terrorist's behavior springs out of a search for identity that can be satisfied only by destroying an enemy.

According to Post, studies of terrorists indicate that they are "action-oriented, aggressive people who are stimulus-hungry and seek excitement."[9] Although it is difficult to prove all terrorists exhibit the same personality quirks, many of them have split personalities resulting from some damage during childhood. A person having such a personality "*splits out* and *projects* onto others all the hatred and devalued weakness within. Individuals who place high reliance on the mechanisms of splitting and externalization look outward for the source of difficulties. They need an outside enemy to blame."[10]

Persons with such backgrounds readily submit to the authoritarianism of terrorist groups, membership in which provides them with a needed sense of support and belonging. In such groups moderation is less respected than the vigorous pursuit of struggle.[11] Post sees a psychological dimension at work here: *"Terrorists whose only sense of significance comes from being terrorists cannot be forced to give up terrorism, for to do so would be to lose their very reason for being."*[12]

Old or New?

Another issue concerning the nature of terrorism is whether it is a form of behavior with a long history or whether it is a comparatively recent development. The tendency to think it is something new is a natural consequence of the fact that the United States has only recently felt its impact on its own shores, in a catastrophe of striking horror. Response to that catastrophe is often referred to as being a "new kind of war," a term that suggests we face a new kind of threat.

Cindy C. Combs is among the scholars who point out that terrorism is not a modern phenomenon. In her book *Terrorism in the Twenty-First Century,* she devotes an entire chapter to pointing this out. According to the account offered by Combs, the term itself originated in the French Revolution even though individual actions that are covered by the term date back to the time of the Roman Empire. The association of religious commitment and violence, which is one of the characteristic dimensions of terrorism, has a long history. Practices such as assassination, privateer piracy, and state-conducted reigns of terror cloud the past of many nations. Guerrilla warfare, which uses selective violence for purposes of insurrection, has a sustained history as well as contemporary expressions. These versions of violence can be discovered even in the story of many states that today would profess to be opposed to terrorism in all its forms. In summary, Combs declares,

> We have established that prior to the twentieth century, terrorism existed in many forms: political assassinations, lethal groups of religious and/or drug crazed murderers and zealots, state-sponsored as well as nonstate pirates, and dedicated revolutionaries whose resort to violence is often tied to state repression. All of these forms of terrorism still exist in the modern world.[13]

Writing in the same vein as Combs, Susan Neiman provides this pithy comment on the events of September 11: "Those who carried out the mass murder on September 11 embodied a form of evil so old-fashioned that its reappearance is part of our shock."[14]

There seems no doubt but that the use of violence to induce fear has a very long history. Hence, it is entirely plausible to regard terrorism as something that bedeviled human experience long before it threatened this generation. Does this mean it makes no sense to speak of terrorism as presenting a new kind of problem? Perhaps the forms and scope of terrorism have recently changed in ways that do warrant thinking of it as something new—or, as Walter Laqueur has named it, "the new terrorism." According to Laqueur,

> Terrorism has been with us for centuries, and it has always attracted inordinate attention because of its dramatic character and sudden, often wholly unexpected, occurrence. It has been a tragedy for the victims, but seen in historical perspective it seldom has been more than a nuisance. Even the bloodiest terrorist incidents in the past . . . affected only a relatively few people. Yesterday's nuisance has become one of the gravest dangers facing mankind. For the first

time in history, weapons of enormous destructive power are
both readily available and harder to track. Science and technology have made enormous progress, but human nature,
alas, has not changed. There is as much fanaticism and
madness as there ever was, and there are now very powerful weapons of mass destruction available to the terrorist.[15]

The dimensions we now confront, not only in the case of
ordinary conflict but also in the case of terrorism, do present
us with a new urgency. What is ironic (perhaps even tragic)
about this situation is that it has been created not by virtue of
what terrorist groups have done in the course of pursuing
their historic tactics, but by virtue of what the major powers—indeed the very major powers that we like to think are
among the more peaceful groups in the world—have done.
The major powers created much of the very weaponry that
now makes terrorism seem to be such a new threat. For example, nuclear weapons were developed by the United States in
the Second World War to offset the possibility that they
would be discovered by nations against which the Allied
powers were fighting. Very few at the time saw the possibility that unleashing a whole new form of destructive potential
would make it possible for a new level of threat to human
well-being to develop outside of control by major political
entities. So great and complicated an endeavor as was
required to make nuclear weapons in the first place made it
almost impossible to realize then that at some point in the
future the results could be appropriated by small groups with
more limited resources than those of nation-states. But
capacities that depend on knowledge are difficult, if not
impossible, to maintain as the sole possession of a single
group. We pulled the nuclear genie out of the bottle through
an enormous effort; terrorists seem now to be on the brink of
picking it up without such enormous logistical capability.

It may not be nuclear capability that makes contemporary
terrorism so threatening as the development of chemical and

biological weaponry. Elementary forms of such weaponry have long been contemplated by many nations and partially developed many years ago. For instance, mustard gas was used in the First World War. But a Geneva protocol of 1925 prohibited the use of such weapons and has been observed with few exceptions until Saddam Hussein violated it during the Iran-Iraq war.[16] Since terrorists are not parties to such agreements either in fact or in spirit, the development of such weapons for massive use does create a possible new dimension to terrorism.

It may be impossible to prevent new groups from acquiring capabilities that have thus been created. As late as 1999 Laqueur wrote, "The technical difficulties standing in the way of the effective use of the arms of mass destructions are still considerable."[17] However, less than four years later an American-led coalition mounted a massive offensive against a country that was believed to be developing such weapons because it was alleged (plausibly or otherwise) that such capabilities could be shared with potential terrorists. We must face the stark possibility that destructive potentials always escalate in ways that make it difficult if not impossible to reverse them or to keep them entirely in the hands of those who develop them. Moreover, in the effort to halt the development of weapons of mass destruction—especially nuclear arms—such weapons might become instruments of last resort and be used by those who have them against those who do not.

Warfare or Crime?

A third antinomy that appears in efforts to think about the nature of terrorism involves the contrast between warfare and crime. Both terms are used in speaking of terrorism. Terrorists themselves often speak of being engaged in a war against their enemies; counterterrorism is often trumpeted to be "a new kind of warfare." The term "war" is used in both cases to suggest the intensity of the effort that is required rather than a particular set of rules or conventions that characterize the ways in which conflict takes place. Used in this way the term "war" signifies an all-out, resolute, total, and essentially unrestricted effort to make opponents behave differently or be destroyed.

But the term "crime" is also used to describe terrorism. For instance, Paul Wilkerson argues that terrorism has essentially criminal features:

> Terrorism is more than simply a manifestation of psycho-pathology and more than a symptom of social discontent, oppression and injustice—though it may be both of these things as well. It is also a moral crime, a crime against humanity, an attack not only on our security, our rule of law, and the safety of the state, but on civilized society itself.[18]

The differences between war and crime are not always crystal clear, but both terms warrant examination in relationship to each other and in relationship to terrorism. Although the nature of armed conflicts that have been designated to be wars has changed over the years, wars have generally been fought for a stated objective following a specific declaration that a state of hostility exists—although the formality of making such a designation has been followed less and less frequently as practice has changed. Wars, even those of recent vintage, have been fought between political sovereignties with the presumption that both sides control the military process and that they can bring a stop to a conflict if negotiations lead to some sort of armistice. Participants in traditional war do not themselves determine the objectives for which they fight, and as individuals are not personally or directly responsible for the conflict. If captured they are neutralized as prisoners of war under international conventions but not regarded as culprits. Moreover, noncombatants are generally protected from attack for moral (or at least humane) reasons. Although this protection has been less and less dependable, it still retains a residual claim as an international convention. Warfare is conducted openly in the sense that the nations involved acknowledge what they are doing and why they are doing it.

Crime, in contrast to war, consists of actions by individuals or small groups who act outside of any official sanction and with as little warning as possible. Such individuals answer only to themselves (or, in the case of organized crime, only to their "bosses"). Crime may be committed for the purpose of gaining some material benefit to which its perpetrators are not entitled, though there are also hate crimes, which occur because people bear grudges or harbor hostility toward certain groups. Those who commit crimes usually seek to avoid being identified as being responsible for having done their malicious work. Criminals are caught and punished (at least hopefully that occurs) rather than made to cease and desist through surrender.

Terrorism has certain features that make it more akin to criminal activity than to war. It is often carried out by some small group that takes the role of antagonist upon itself. Terrorism is usually carried out without the support and backing of a specific political sovereignty, or if that support is involved it is often from behind the scenes and unacknowledged. It is difficult to predict when, where, or at whom terrorists will strike. Those who engage in terrorist activities are personally committed to the cause, do not officially identify themselves as combatants, and are not necessarily subject to the control of any political entity that can require them to surrender if a settlement is negotiated. The traditional assumption that noncombatants enjoy immunity from attack is entirely jettisoned. Indeed, attacks on civilians are the primary way in which terrorists make themselves felt. As in the case of hate crimes, terrorism is often an expression of discontent or hatred that flays out in hostile anger. Moreover, terrorists do not wear uniforms to identify themselves as combatants. Terrorism is an outlaw or "nonlaw" activity carried out by persons who cannot readily be identified and who act as relatively small units that have to be caught and apprehended on a one-to-one basis if they are to be stopped.

The characterization of terrorism as crime has been central in actions taken by the international community over a period of many years. Several treaties have been made that define terrorism as a "crime against humanity," and almost every one of the actions that terrorists use are covered by this designation. The Security Council of the United Nations has repeatedly designated terrorism as a crime. This position was reaffirmed in Resolution 1377 adopted November 12, 2001. With this declaration the Security Council reaffirmed

> its unequivocal condemnation of all acts, methods, and practices of terrorism as criminal and unjustifiable, regardless of their intention, in all their forms and manifestations, wherever and by whomever committed.

But there are also ways in which terrorism differs from crime. Criminals are usually seeking some personal gain or advantage—to acquire some "loot"—from their efforts. Terrorists do their thing more for ideological or political (or religious) reasons. Many terrorists are oblivious to the fear of being attacked or destroyed because they may even welcome the prospect of dying for their cause. Like covert action, terrorism depends on stealth rather than acknowledged intentions, on unpredictability rather than regular planned campaigns, on the capacity to disrupt infrastructures rather than to defeat a clearly identified opponent. Many criminals seek to minimize violence, to obtain their objectives with the least serious damage to those who might be in the way. Most terrorists see the doing of harm as central to their activity, not incidental to it. Terrorism is probably more like so-called hate crimes or capital offenses in its possible motivation than like robberies or embezzlements.

The interrelationship between terrorism and war is illuminated by looking at how terrorism compares to deterrence. Both operate by inducing fear. Deterrence uses the threat to destroy as a means of keeping other parties from doing certain things. Terrorism sometimes uses the threat to destroy as a means to get people to do things they might not otherwise be willing to do. Both assume that the creation of fear is a powerful tool for achieving certain consequences. Deterrence belongs to the realm of warfare; insofar as terrorism shares certain features with deterrence it also belongs to the realm of warfare.

Because terrorism has some features that make it like warfare and other features that make it like crime, it is difficult to describe it as belonging to either sphere by itself. It is also a reason to suspect that no strategy of counterterrorism built only on one model—either the model of war or the model of crime suppression—will be sufficient to bring it under control. The war model by itself will not suffice because it is unlikely that the day will come when terrorism ceases to exist because terrorists have agreed to an armistice as a result of having been successfully defeated by superior force. The criminal justice model by itself will not suffice because it relies on the use of sanctions that terrorists do not fear because the commitment to their cause goes way beyond self-interest. This makes terrorism a very formidable type of malfeasance.

What Terrorism Is Not

If, as noted at the beginning of this chapter, the term terrorism is applied to many kinds of violence and used more as an expression of disapproval than as a description of a particular kind of behavior, then it is important to indicate what the term does not mean. This is only a bit less difficult than trying to indicate what it does mean.

The term does not refer to insurrections that arise from justified grievances against oppressive regimes. The United States was born by engaging in such an action, then called a revolution. The Boston Tea Party might have terrified the British, but it was not a form of terrorism. Today such actions are often called "wars of liberation." These may or may not warrant support, depending on the particulars of the case and the moral assumptions of those contemplating whether or not to offer aid. To be sure, it is possible that wars of liberation may become intertwined with terrorist strategies, but it would only be the particular forms of behavior that mark terrorism that should be thus described, not the resort to force for the purposes of overthrowing tyranny or oppression.

Similarly, the term terrorism does not apply to guerilla warfare—that is, violence openly used selectively by small groups against military targets. In the end, it may not be possible to keep the distinctions clear in practice as easily as they can be separated in writing.

> Revolutions are not by definition terrorist events. Indeed, some have been successfully carried out without resort to terrorist tactics. It is increasingly difficult, however, for an untrained and sparsely equipped indigenous army to wage a successful guerilla war against a standing national army. With mounting frustration in the face of apparently insurmountable odds, it is increasingly easy to resort to terror-violence to achieve by psychological force what is not possible to achieve by force of arms.[19]

Most clearly, civil disobedience, despite the possible disruption that it may cause, is not a form of terrorism. Especially when, as is usually the case, it is committed to nonviolence, it cannot be even remotely considered to pose the issues that terrorism does. Likewise, "sit-ins, picket lines, walkouts, and other similar forms of protest, no matter how destructive, are *not* terrorist acts."[20]

A Focus That Refocuses

All this having been considered, it may be possible to bring the discussion of what terrorism is to something of a focus, albeit not to a consensus. Combs offers her suggestion for doing this with the following description of terrorism:

> [Terrorism] *is a synthesis of war and theatre, a dramatization of the most proscribed kind of violence—that which is perpetrated on innocent victims—played before an audience in the hope of creating a mood of fear, for political purposes.*[21]

This definition certainly covers many of the events and practices that are so disturbing, and it highlights many of the special features that differentiate terrorism from other forms of violence. But it also presents a most sobering possibility. Would this definition not also include the way in which the United States ended the Second World War with an unannounced destruction of two Japanese cities? The use of the atomic bomb on innocent victims was done for demonstration purposes. While it was part of a war, and the citizens of Hiroshima and Nagasaki might not be considered innocent victims because their country was at war, that consideration does not offer decisive refutation of the possibility that this was a terrorist action. Although Alan Dershowitz does not carry this point to such a conclusion, he does indicate the problem it raises if terrorism is characterized mainly as an attack on innocent bystanders.[22] It does not quite suffice to simply say that few people would consider that action to be terrorist in nature, or to suggest it was not such because the United States did it and the United States is a peace-loving nation, or to argue that because it was connected with a war it was therefore legitimate. The destruction of those two cities involved a massive use of unprecedented power aimed at essentially innocent people for purposes of demonstrating they should surrender.

Perhaps we need to refocus the agenda of this whole discussion. It has been concerned to define what terrorism is. This effort has proceeded on the assumption that it is for us to define the term and decide what terrorism is and why it is unacceptable. But perhaps we should ask how terrorism defines the present world and us as part of that world. Terrorism reveals what human beings have become. Terrorism reveals the extent to which reliance upon violence has become a continuing and central feature of modern life that affects the behavior of everybody, not merely a few malicious actors bent on doing some new evil. It indicates the extent to which we have all been sucked into a vortex of violence that shapes much of our contemporary experience. If that is the case, the task before us is to reverse that whole process and everything that has contributed to it rather than merely to take upon ourselves a stance of righteous indignation that propels us toward the ever greater use of violence to rid the world of those whose way of using violence we disapprove of.

Chapter 2

The Causes of Terrorism

Coming to a clear idea about the causes of terrorism is just as difficult as obtaining agreement about the nature of terrorism. Terrorism arises for numerous and complex reasons. Explanations made from one perspective are often completely at odds with explanations made from another perspective. The disagreements that arise from different ways of explaining why terrorism has developed into a major threat are frequently charged with emotion. Hard-nosed realism often lines up against moral idealism, national self-interest against prophetic self-criticism. The debates never seem to reach closure. Hawks see matters one way; doves see matters quite differently. There are very few owls.

This chapter, therefore, is not likely to offer an explanation for the causes of terrorism that every reader will find convincing. Perhaps, however, it can suggest where the disagreements lie, offer insights that are not always brought to light in "sound bite" presentations, and suggest ways of making the examination of the issues more enlightening. Those who believe that terrorism stems directly from the perverse and malicious evildoing of rogue leaders will not be convinced by the arguments of those who believe it has understandable causes—even causes that stem to a considerable measure from the way in which the major powers have conducted themselves in world affairs.

It may be that only fools, not owls, take on such matters. But they are not to be treated with jest, for they are serious and complex issues, occasions of momentous agony, and a source of deep frustration. Nevertheless, they must be addressed, if only to clarify why they bring forth such glaring and seemingly persistent disagreements. Why are wisdom and good intentions so often stymied in the effort to understand such matters? Perhaps it is because, as postmodernists hold, all perceptions are determined by the standing ground of those who do the thinking. If that is the case, no analysis of problems can be done apart from the prior ideological stances or the convictions people bring to the analysis. This means that all attempts to make explanations are merely rationalizations of judgments already made. But rather than conceding that to be entirely the case, it is worth trying to look at the differences and to see if they offer clues. Maybe fools can help us think about things in ways that hawks and doves and even owls may not.

In the material that follows, possible explanations for the resurgence of terrorism are grouped under three headings. The first group looks at the possible political factors that may cause terrorism—factors that are based in the policies and attitudes of various actors in world affairs. The second group looks at changes that have taken place in the way international conflict has been conducted in recent decades—changes that provide a context for the rise of terrorism. Finally, the chapter deals with the vexing and not fully understood relationship between religion and violence in the hope that it may be possible to discern some of the reasons why traditions that profess to be dedicated to peace and compassion are often the sources of conflict and hatred.

Political and Economic Factors

The last half of the twentieth century was a turbulent era, a time overshadowed for several decades by the Cold War, which pitted two major powers armed with nuclear weapons against each other in a standoff that constantly threatened to break out into open hostility. Each of these powers maintained a level of military preparedness that would have had disastrous consequences if used. Each of the major powers maneuvered in world affairs in order to bolster its position over the other. Because resort to the use of the ultimate weapon was "unthinkable" (though plenty of thinking went on about it), each of the major powers made alliances with other groups around the world that could help it to maintain a balance of power. This was done under the aegis of realist thinking of the type that reduces international dynamics to matters of power. Realists of this type—perhaps legitimately dubbed reductionistic realists—were often successful in persuading the major powers that they could make alliances without scruples as to the political and moral stances of those from whom they could gain support. For instance, at one point the United States actually supported both Saddam Hussein and the Taliban because it saw them as effective allies in the effort to restrain Soviet power.

Those examples strike home with special intensity because we have subsequently found ourselves in conflict with these very same parties. But this is only one example of a kind of diplomatic and military strategy followed by the United States for the entire length of the Cold War. These moves came into ever increasing use because it was widely argued that the failure to take power seriously was the most likely way in which to invite attacks against one's vital interests. Realists believe that to be weak, or to appear to be weak, is to lose influence and invite disaster. They are far less sensitive to the correlative phenomenon that to be strong and to flaunt power is to invite resentment.

To be sure, the United States has done many generous things in the world since the end of the Second World War. It helped rebuild the nations that were defeated; it has offered aid to some needy nations; it has come to the aid of countries that have been the targets of aggression by others or that have been racked by turmoil within. Why then should its behavior have produced something of a backlash? It may be that people are generally more prone to resent the use of power than to appreciate the benefits of bestowed assistance. For instance, on the personal or local level they are more likely to be agitated by threats to their homes or safety than to be appreciative of all the many benefits and conveniences that government provides. On the level of world affairs, there is no doubt but that American power, now without equivalent to that of any other nation, is a dominant feature of contemporary world affairs. That scares others, potential antagonists and even friends. Power is more likely to be resented than benevolence is to be appreciated. Power creates empire, even when it does not intend to do so and even when it does not seek to dominate every other nation. Michael Ignatieff describes the new American empire:

> America's empire is not like empires of times past, built on colonies, conquest, and the white man's burden. We are no longer in the era of the United Fruit Company, when American corporations needed the Marines to secure their investments overseas. The 21st century imperium is a new invention in the annals of political science, an empire lite, a global hegemony whose grace notes are free markets, human rights, and democracy enforced by the most awesome military power the world has ever known. It is the imperialism of a people who remember that their country secured its independence by revolt against an empire, and who like to think of themselves as the friend of free-

dom everywhere. It is an empire without consciousness of itself as such, constantly shocked that its good intentions arouse resentment abroad. But that does not make it any less of an empire, with a conviction that it alone, in Herman Melville's words "bears the ark of the liberties of the world."[1]

Although this may be the large picture, something of an enigma or a paradox, there are other factors that have to be acknowledged in order to understand the possible roots of terrorism as a response to political factors. The use of power can be self-serving as well as benevolent. Shifting for the moment from the Middle East to South America, it is important to realize that the United States has sometimes done things very contrary to its professed ideals. In Colombia and other countries, it has put its weight behind governments that maintain the status quo by repressive methods. At the School of the Americas (now called WHISC, or Western Hemisphere Institute for Security Cooperation) in Fort Benning, Georgia, it has even provided training for military actions that bear a mighty close resemblance to what terrorists do.[2] This operation has been criticized by church groups and others, and has been picketed by resisters who have sometimes gone to jail for violations of trespassing laws.[3] However, these kinds of actions have continued and thereby given plausible evidence to those who argue that the behavior of the United States in the exercise of its military power contributes to the conditions out of which terrorism arises. If this country trains persons for covert violence in one part of the world, what is the moral ground for its condemnation of terrorism in other parts of the world?

Let us return to the Middle East. This is a place of political turmoil and deep unrest. In a profound way it is the most fertile seedbed of violence in the world—terrorism that has developed in opposition to the state of Israel and the random strikes employed in efforts to protect it. The creation of Israel displaced Palestinians from land they considered to be their own. To be sure, Jews as a group have been visited upon by calamities and oppression beyond imagining—not least because they lived for so long without a homeland under their own control. Their desire for a homeland is understandable, for political security involves geography as well as legislation, a secure place as well as favorable policy. But to obtain these benefits by taking them away from others is to invite enduring conflict. When that conflict cannot be, or is not, resolved by other means, it invites the rise of terrorism. Such terrorism may be less a means of obtaining a different ordering of the political situation than a way of expressing bitter discontent with the present state of affairs. But that may make it even harder to deal with.

There are political dimensions to many of the other instances of terrorism in our contemporary world. But America has not sided as clearly with one side in the other cases as it has sided with Israel. It has not defended one side in the conflict between Protestants or Catholics in Ireland, or between the Sikhs and the government of India. It did not become involved when members of the Aum Shinrikyo released poison in the subways of Tokyo. There are political dimensions to those uses of terrorism as well, but we have not become involved to the same extent as we have become involved in defending Israel against the terrorism that has been directed at it. Moreover, in the case of Israel the retaliatory strikes it has employed to deter the terrorist attacks are not without some of the very features of unpredictable and theatrical violence that mark terrorism. This probably explains why the terrorism that is most likely to threaten the United States comes from the Middle East.

The political factors that have contributed to discontent with the dominance of Western, particularly American, influence in the world are interwoven with economic factors that exacerbate the resentment and distrust. Economic conditions in those parts of the world that are dominated by the economic outreach of trade and commerce from the powerful nations have not shown adequate progress in overcoming poverty. Many of the policies and programs that have been aimed at doing so have, whether intentionally or not, sometimes served privilege rather than alleviated poverty. In many cases the policies and behavior of transnational corporations has affected the welfare of people in the third world more decisively that the policies of nation-states. Such policies have not always been as attentive to matters of justice overseas as they are required (primarily by social legislation) to be in first world settings. Even if the economic aspect of globalization has worked to the betterment of peoples in the third world (a matter much debated), the disparity between their lot and those of people in the countries with power and affluence remains a glaring contrast.

In a general audience a year after the attacks of September 11, Pope John Paul II made comments that indicate he believes that terrorism is caused by political and economic factors. Expressing concern for the victims of the attack, and strongly condemning terrorism as a way to redress grievances, the pope nevertheless wrote that

> an agreed upon and resolute effort is necessary and urgent to advance new political and economic initiatives that are capable of resolving the scandalous situations of injustice and oppression that continue to afflict a great many of the members of the human family, creating conditions that favor the uncontrollable explosion of rancor. When fundamental rights are violated, it is easy to fall prey to the temptations of hatred and violence.[4]

If political and economic factors alone account for terrorism it would be possible to argue that if only the United States had behaved differently in the world, if it had refrained from the opportunistic power politics it has played, if it had not sided with those it did not approve to counter the power of those it vehemently disapproved, if it had not trained people to do terrorist-like acts in situations in which it had an interest, if it had not acquired the status of an empire, if in extending their commercial activities American companies had treated the people in other countries with the same concern for just compensation as Americans expect, we might not be faced with the contemporary threat of terrorism. Although there may be some truth to this conclusion, it is impossible to prove. If, of course, international politics were an arena in which sober people made entirely pragmatic judgments based on good intentions and governed by moral principles, that alternative might be conceivable, but international politics are such a complex mix of rationality and emotion, of strategic calculation and reactive fervor that it is problematic to think that international affairs can be conducted in ways that please all parties. To have behaved differently might have made matters better, but it cannot be argued it would have made things altogether different. There is no way of proving that political miscalculation alone bears the entire onus for terrorism.

Contextual Factors

The discussion now turns to another set of factors that bear upon the rise of terrorism, factors that involve changes in the way violence has come to be practiced in warfare. Although "war" remains the common designation for hostilities between large groups (such as nation-states or alliances of nation-states), the actions that are signified by the term underwent significant developments and transformations in the twentieth century. Similarly, political and moral thinking about war has changed as the characteristics, extent, and prevalence of conflict have changed. These changes are not without significance for understanding why terrorism has arisen.

The First World War was considered by many, in the words of Woodrow Wilson, to be a "war to make the world safe for democracy." It was fought largely by ground troops commissioned for combat roles by nations declaring their intentions to use force for political purposes. The conflict was fought on the battlefield by the armies of sovereign states pitted against each other. Airplanes were just coming into use and were employed to sweep soldiers from their positions. "Dog fights" between pilots from opposing sides occurred in the air, but did not endanger noncombatants to any significant extent. The United States understood itself as helping the European allies fight an enemy that posed a threat to their security. The moral atmosphere prevalent during the First World War was characterized by a sharp and clear distinction between the righteousness of one side and the evil of the other. Support for the war was widespread and without qualifying reservations. The armistice that followed was essentially punitive. Such features are characteristic of a crusade—an ethic of conflict in which it is assumed that it is the moral obligation of the righteous to bring evildoers to abject submission, if not, indeed, to destroy them completely.

Following the armistice, efforts to establish a League of Nations to deal with future conflicts met with only limited success and did not have the support of the United States. As it became apparent over the course of time that the war and the armistice had failed to make the world more democratic, a rather widespread, but by no means dominant, pacifism arose in the mainline churches. This pacifism was embraced as a politically relevant option. It held that by opposing the use of force, the chance of resorting to war as a solution for international disputes would be diminished. Although grounded on very different premises, this pacifist thinking tended to team up with political isolationism, which argued against becoming entangled in international disputes.

The United States first became involved in the Second World War by giving aid to the Allies. The pacifist/isolationist mood that followed the First World War slowly gave way to the realization that totalitarian regimes represented a grave threat to Western values. However, America's full involvement began only when Pearl Harbor was attacked. While ground and sea combat still played a significant role in military operations, the Second World War brought forth the major use of air power, not only as a tool for use in theaters of combat but as a means of destroying the infrastructures of the enemy. The bombing of cities that occurred violated the just war principle of noncombatant immunity, and obliteration bombing came to be regarded as an acceptable means of waging war. Respect for the principle of noncombatant immunity was completely ignored when the war was suddenly concluded after the destruction of two whole cities with the use of nuclear bombs—an action taken without any warning that could have allowed Japan to surrender.

Christian thinking about the morality of the Second World War was divided. Pacifism continued to be embraced by a considerable group,[5] but it did not constitute a source of strong opposition to the war. Many, perhaps a majority, realized the war to be necessary but nevertheless morally troubling, and often spoke of the war as "hell, not sin."[6] The resulting moral stance may be described as "agonized participation."[7] The crusading stance evident in the First World War receded into the background because even those agonized participants who felt the war to be necessary were fully aware that military force by itself is a tragic and ultimately inadequate way to produce an enduring solution to the problems of international misdoing.

Although the Second World War was fought under the banner of seeking "unconditional surrender" (a remnant of crusade thinking), the making of the subsequent peace included provision for rehabilitating the defeated nations. A great deal of thinking—much of it done under religious auspices—went on during the war, pointing to the conditions necessary to create a "just and durable peace."[8] Such thinking may have helped to avoid the retributive mood that followed the First World War and to prevent the goal of unconditional surrender from resulting in the abject humiliation of the defeated nations. Moreover, there was a growing and widespread view that some sort of international organization should be created; this thinking led to the formation of the United Nations.

One outgrowth of this conflict was the Nuremberg trials, which brought to justice a few high-level individuals who had shown particularly horrendous behavior during the war. These individuals were brought before a judicial panel for war crimes. Although the principle of individual accountability for behavior in times of war was not entirely new, it was given a considerable new importance by these trials. The legitimacy of these procedures was questioned, both by those who considered them too vindictive and by those who were concerned that they would establish precedents which could in the future endanger officials of sovereign nations who carried out their country's policies in reasonably good faith.[9] These trials were significant because they advanced the principle that individuals may be responsible when they violate basic standards of human decency, even if they do so in conformity to the policies of their own nation-state.

The war in Korea came relatively soon on the heels of the Second World War. It was the first war in history in which troops accountable to a world organization were used to stem an act of aggression. This was sometimes called "police action." Because the war involved the principle of collective security it garnered considerable support from liberals anxious for world government to be effective. Yet it was questioned by some conservatives because it was pursued on a limited basis to stop aggression rather than as an effort to defeat an enemy decisively. The warrant for the Korean War was less convincing to super hawks than to hesitant doves. The conflict was over before any major theological and moral stances developed about the use of military means for policing purposes, although some of the factors that go into just war thinking were implicit in the controversy about the suitability of conducting war on a limited basis.

The war in Vietnam started as an operation to deal with circumstances similar to those confronted in Korea, but was undertaken as an action by the United States to stem the spread of communism in Southeast Asia. At the start it was hoped it would be a similarly controlled response. But it became a logistical and strategic nightmare for a number of complex reasons. The conflict was marked by intense local ground combat that air power could not replace. Media coverage of the war, bringing into almost every home the awareness of conflict's horror, did much to diminish patriotic fervor and the glorification of heroism. The result was an intense and divisive public controversy about the legitimacy of the war—a controversy without precedent in modern times and one that greatly eroded the traditional support for military action that had been relatively constant during most of the earlier conflicts in this century. Controversy over the Vietnam War brought just war theory into explicit use as a basis for making the case against the legitimacy of a particular conflict. For instance, in a background paper prepared by a task force of Presbyterians, this judgment was stated bluntly: "Only inhumane and internationally dangerous techniques of social attrition and obliteration warfare could 'win' the Vietnam war militarily. These would be utterly unjust (indiscriminate and disproportionate) means."[10]

Both the war in Korea and the war in Vietnam were part of the Cold War. The Cold War was marked by reliance upon deterrence, that is, the possession of massive power (primarily nuclear) that was held as a means of creating fear in any opposing power (as well as in any potentially opposing powers) that would keep it (or them) from resorting to armed aggression to achieve their goals. The nuclear arms race between two major powers was the subject of considerable moral concern and drew criticism from many sources. After many years of discussion and debate such opposition culminated in major pronouncements by two major Christian groups and less publicized resolutions by others.[11] These statements argued that the possible use of nuclear arms is morally unacceptable because of the high potential for indiscriminate destruction. Although these statements came from the leadership of mainline religious bodies with a presumed moral influence and a previous history of support for the nation when at war, it is unlikely they did much to change the reliance of the major powers on nuclear weapons for massive retaliation. However, they did further the use of just war considerations in the public debate.

The Cuban crisis, which involved nuclear brinkmanship at the height of the Cold War, was probably the instance in which the tenuous standoff between the major parties at loggerheads came closest to resulting in destructive combat. Meanwhile, in other places, local conflicts arose and sometimes enabled the major parties to advance their interests without coming to a full and complete confrontation. Wars of national liberation took place, greatly escalating the use of insurgency tactics and prompting the development of covert actions as a new way of resisting such violence. Covert action seemed to provide a strategy by which nations might be involved in conflicts without having to declare themselves participants and without having to assume the burdens and obligations associated with being formally committed to a war. Covert action could also bypass the obligations imposed by the conventions of international law that had been drawn up over the years to keep the conduct of war restrained. The United States used covert action in several parts of the world

JUST WAR CRITERIA

Christian teaching about just war is formulated a bit differently by various authorities but always presupposes that war may be supported only for special and weighty moral reasons. It provides criteria for deciding, first, under what circumstances it is legitimate to use armed conflict and, second, what restraints on that use are required for warfare to be morally acceptable. One of the most recent and succinct formulations sets forth these conditions as follows:

> 1) The cause itself must be just—to right a wrong, to defend against acts of aggression, to protect the innocent from injury, etc.; 2) it must be undertaken by legitimate authority, thus confirming and strengthening responsible political order; 3) it must be a last resort, undertaken only after every reasonable measure short of war has been found inadequate; 4) its reasonably predictable consequences must be better than the consequences of not going to war. That is, the good attained or the evil resisted must be proportional to the evil of war itself; 5) there must be reasonable expectation of victory; 6) in the actual conduct of war, the belligerents must maintain "right intention," that is, always desiring peace with justice, never seeking unjust gains, not being corrupted by hatred, while remaining open to reconciliation; and 7) the means used must be consistent with the just purpose, there can be no directly intended injury to non-combatants. (From "Christians and War in the 21st Century," *Shalom Papers: A Journal of Theology and Public Policy* 5, no. 1 [2003], 12–13. My own formulation of these conditions can be found in *War and Conscience in America* [Philadelphia: Westminster Press, 1968], 21–33.)

to deal with trouble spots without having to engage in conflict openly.

When Iraq invaded Kuwait in 1990, President Bush condemned the action as outrageous and brutal. The first strategy was to use economic sanctions as a way to restrain Iraq, though some observers believe these were adopted only as a delaying action to permit the buildup of sufficient military forces to defeat Iraq on the battlefield. Subsequently, Bush went to the United Nations to obtain a mandate for taking action against Iraq as a responsibility of the United States. The United Nations at the time had been weakened by the failure of the United States to pay its dues and accord it an important function, and it did not have peacekeeping capacities. Debates took place in the administration itself, in the Congress, and in the nation about the wisdom of these moves, but the outcome was to engage Iraq militarily with an international coalition dominated by the United States.

The Gulf War was relatively short. Air power played a dominant role, and highly sophisticated "smart bombs" were used in large numbers for the first time, which were portrayed as permitting the discrimination between military targets and civilian sites. This war was concluded with relatively few casualties among U.S. forces. Since the draft was eliminated in the 1970s and the armed forces filled its ranks with volunteers, the issue of conscientious objection was minimized.

Thinking by religious bodies about the issues posed by this war never coalesced into a discernible consensus, though much of it was critical. However, whereas in the case of Vietnam those who used just war criteria were opposed to the conflict, in the case of the Gulf War the Bush administration explicitly invoked just war criteria to legitimize its decisions (though critics of those decisions also used just war categories to make their case). This demonstrated that just war teaching is context specific and does not necessarily yield agreement on the moral legitimacy or illegitimacy of any specific conflict. It tends to be a tool for use in debate rather than an instrument that yields moral agreement.[12]

Alongside of, or as an integral part of, several of these conflicts, economic sanctions of came to be employed as instruments of diplomatic and military pressure. Since imposing sanctions can be accomplished with minimal risks to the personnel of the nations that impose them, they appear to be less costly and destructive than overt forms of conflict. But sanctions can create major hardships on civilians and civilian infrastructures (in contrast to wartime sieges aimed only at specific military installations) and therefore can pose serious moral issues for the requirements of noncombatant immunity—a point that has been recognized by more thoughtful commentators but largely overlooked by the public. Sanctions adversely affect the innocent even if they do not involve overt violence, and therefore their use contributes to a general trend to ignore the need to protect noncombatants from harm.

A late development in twentieth-century conflict was the use of military power for the purpose of humanitarian intervention. This was undertaken to maintain order in places where the rule of law had broken down, or where the populations of certain areas had suffered horrendous dislocations and lethal threats. Humanitarian intervention requires the crossing of national boundaries (even if not explicitly invited to do so) in order to alleviate suffering. In the case of most interventions by the United Nations, the consent of the parties has been given. The practice has been the subject of major criticism, but humanitarian intervention enjoys widespread appeal. However, this may be so for idealistic reasons rather than the result of adequate analysis with careful moral reasoning.[13] Perhaps the most significant consequence of the development of humanitarian intervention has been to raise the possibility of breaching the sovereignty of individual nations whose internal affairs do not measure up to the task of ensuring human rights or supporting a minimally adequate level of human well-being for the people within their borders.

The foregoing developments have created several trends that provide a context for the development of terrorism. Obviously, these trends have not directly caused terrorism to develop, but they have created conditions in which it could arise.

First, these developments have increasingly brought the theater of military action closer and closer to the life of ordinary people whose homes and lives have been targets of air-delivered weaponry on an ever escalating level of destructiveness. This development may have been alleviated recently to a very small extent by the employment of so-called smart bombs. Although such bombs are more accurate in finding their target, they are also more lethal and do not entirely overcome the problem of civilian casualties. Overall, the main movement of warfare from battlefield to infrastructure has been momentous. Until September 11, 2001, the people of the United States had not felt this change as much as people in many other parts of the world. Terrorism has developed within this widening sphere of military action in which distinctions between soldiers and civilians are less clearly observed.

Second, conflict has developed forms in which those engaged in military actions are not necessarily at risk to the same extent as they were in traditional forms of conflict. Technology has made it possible to deliver increased destruction at decreased risk. Covert action has created modes of conflict that need not be "owned up to" by those who engage in them. The ties between political responsibility and the conduct of war that has been a central premise in much of the past and that undergirds traditional just war thinking have become increasingly tenuous. Such developments in the conduct of war are but steps along the way to terrorism.

Third, national sovereignty in decision making about conflict has been subtly, yet significantly, modified. Not only have some decisions come to be deemed appropriate for the nations to make together (as through the United Nations), but there has been an increasing tendency to hold rulers accountable for their behavior by commonly acknowledged standards that are not to be bracketed out because such behavior occurs under the cloak of national sovereignty. Moreover, nation-states no longer enjoy a complete presumption of the right to do whatever they please within their borders or in the treatment of other nations. But while this development can have positive implications for international cooperation, it also means that nations may no longer have the same control over what is done within their borders or under their auspices as they once did, and that terrorists do not necessarily regard their identification with any particular nations as providing a decisive restraint over their behavior.

Fourth, the twentieth century saw war and preparation to fight war become an ongoing aspect of statecraft. The capacity to carry on conflict has become a permanent feature of governments on a heightened scale, and preparedness for war a permanent necessity. Instead of military power being viewed as something that is geared up when diplomacy fails, military power has become a primary ingredient in diplomacy. In order to mount deterrence effectively and to maintain it indefinitely, nations have become more or less permanently mobilized for military purposes. The central feature of this permanent preparedness is deterrence. Terrorism relies on the same capacity to induce fear as does deterrence. When the use of force becomes the normal way to think about statecraft, the embrace of terrorism ceases to be quite as unthinkable as it once was.

Religious Factors

This discussion must now turn to the most difficult and perhaps least anticipated cause of terrorism—its rootage in religious faith and practice. There can be no doubt but that terrorism makes the connection between religion and violence apparent. The connection is prevalent and inescapable. How can that feature of human behavior which often professes to foster peace and compassion be the source of violence? John R. Hall observes that the very fact religion is held up as a vessel of peace has done much to keep social theorists from paying attention to its relationship to violence.[14] Moreover, the adherents of various faith traditions have not been anxious to acknowledge the extent to which the practice of religion is often a source of very destructive behavior. Biting the bullet on this matter may be like biting the apple in the story of the fall—an awakening to the nakedness of our thinking. This is not appealing sermon material for churches that look to religion as a source of blessedness.

The connection between religion and violence occurs in almost every tradition. Mark Juergensmeyer has studied with impressive thoroughness instances of terrorism around the world.[15] In the great majority of cases these have been exacerbated by close relation to religion. Instances of purely secular terrorism are relatively few and far between. Nor do these various terrorist activities stem only from one tradition. They represent a more universal pattern, the most characteristic feature of which may very well be their connection to religion. To realize that is sobering, even disconcerting, especially to those of us who have long cherished religion for its commitment to peace and goodwill.

While it is important to recognize the existence of a connection between religion and violence especially as that connection is manifested in terrorism, that alone will not suffice. Although it is difficult to do so, and the theoretical work available is limited, we must inquire about the causal relationships that are involved. Juergensmeyer makes several suggestions that offer a helpful beginning for the following considerations.[16] Religion and terrorism have certain common features.

They both are theatrical; neither religion nor terrorism would gain much attention without being so. They both need audiences. They both engage in something that might be called a ritual, that is, an action that bears meaning beyond what it actually achieves. They therefore deal in symbolism—using behavior for purposes that have significance beyond the specific accomplishments that are achieved by the action itself. Instead of mounting modest programs to advance human well-being incrementally, much religion and much terrorism place an aura of ultimacy around their behavior—or, as Juergensmeyer puts it, give their agendas a cosmic dimension:

> What makes religious violence particularly savage and relentless is that its perpetrators have placed such religious images of the divine struggle—cosmic war—in the service of worldly political battles. For this reason, acts of religious terror serve not only as tactics in a political strategy but also as evocations of a much larger spiritual confrontation.[17]

Much religion and much terrorism are alike in that they extol the virtues of struggle as a value in itself. They prompt resolves that produce sacrificial effort, that honor commitment that exceeds prudence, that make sacrifice itself a mark of virtue.

In all violence, whether undertaken for purposes of aggression or used as a way to stem aggression, there has always been a risk of injury or death. Religion has frequently provided courage to those who face the possibility of death by offering the assurance that life in time and on earth is not the only reality. In the case of terrorism this assurance is extended, not merely to provide courage to face the possibility of death but to provide a motive for deliberatively choosing to die. The idea of martyrdom is a religiously grounded idea; indeed, it functions with effectiveness only when entertained in a religious context. Religion blesses martyrdom as a form of sacrifice. This is not pernicious when the sacrifice is accepted by those who seek to be faithful to their beliefs out of their purity of heart (though as Thomas à Becket, in T. S. Eliot's play *Murder in the Cathedral*, helps us to see, keeping that intention free of the desire for self-vindication is not always easy). In terrorism the acceptance of martyrdom overrides even the strong religious disapproval of suicide. Moreover, it undercuts the assumptions behind and beneath all uses of violence—namely, that people will change their behavior or submit to capture rather than lose their lives. There are few, if any, secular counterparts to this way of thinking. Bizarre and disturbing though it is, it cannot be understood except in terms of a religious dynamic gone amok.

A prevalent modern view of religion sees it as an aspect of morality that inspires noble living. This view assumes religion to be a source of behavioral guidance. But religion is also a source of power—not physical power as much as psychic power.[18] As a source of power, religion provides the impetus for behavior—an impetus that can bolster either noble or demonic actions. Religions can make just and compassionate people more noble than they would be without embracing it; conversely, it can make others more truculent and arrogant. Some have suggested that Christians ought not to think of their faith as a form of religion, in order that the human striving and brittle harshness that are possible when religion intensifies malfeasance can be repudiated. While well intentioned, these proposals for espousing faith as a nonreligious entity have not been altogether persuasive and have not been widely understood. Nevertheless, they do highlight a very perplexing feature of religion—that it is a form of power that makes goodness more possible but also runs the risk of intensifying dangerous and unacceptable behavior. In terrorism we see an unsettling demonstration of the latter possibility.

There is still a deeper level on which the connection of religion and violence can be understood. According to Rene Girard, the practice and embrace of religion involves the practice and embrace of violence. Sacrifice, a prominent feature of religion, involves violence; rituals of passage are often painful if not altogether cruel. They are used to keep change from disturbing the status quo.[19] Religion provides a surrogate victim for the violence by which institutional life is maintained. "All man's religious, familial, economic and social institutions grew out of the body of an original victim."[20] While those who embrace religion may not sense the extent to which the very framework of their worldview involves the presence of violence, that fact is nevertheless there as a sobering reality, as something that cannot be dismissed as merely incidental. Modern thinking has sought to deny the close connection between the sacred and the violent and hence has created a crisis. "This crisis is similar but not identical to previous ones. We have managed to extricate ourselves from the sacred somewhat more successfully than other societies have done, to the point of losing all memory of the generative violence, but we are about to rediscover it."[21]

Faced with such a theory and the possibility that terrorism could be forcing us to rediscover something we have laid aside, we are likely to recoil—denying vociferously its import and claiming exemption from the realities to which it points. As in the case of terrorism, we are likely to see the dimensions of violence only in the religions of others, not in that which we embrace. But certain theories of the atonement imply that violence is closely intertwined with redemption. The struggle against capital punishment is still resisted by many American Christians. Advocacy of nonviolence as a moral imperative still faces enormous resistance from religious people. Terrorism demonstrates the link between religion and violence. On what ground can any of us prove that we do not make the same linkage?

Chapter 3

Models for Countering Terrorism

*T*hose who recognize that terrorism poses a threat do not necessarily agree how best to counter it. If, as has been pointed out in the first two chapters, terrorism is difficult to define and stems from a variety of causes, countering terrorism will not be simple, quick, or easy. Yet the very nature of the terrorist threat and the fact that it has brought violence to the continental United States creates an understandable impatience, a mood to deal with the threat decisively and without equivocation. Noting this impulse, a scholar who has considered these matters at length has observed that a

> prevalent pattern of thinking and discussion about counterterrorism is a tendency toward absolute solutions and a rejection of accommodation and finesse. If counterterrorism is conceived as a war, it is a very small step to conclude that in this war there is no substitute for victory and thus no room for compromise. The nature of terrorism and of how American public attention to it has evolved in recent years have made the topic prone to this simplistic pattern of thought. Americans have had little reason to come to terms with the causes or issues associated with the terrorism that has struck closest to their home and been emblazoned most prominently in the newspapers and their memories. They have had more reason to think of terrorism simply as an evil

to be eradicated, rather than a more complex phenomenon
with sides that may need to be reckoned with differently.[1]

This passage rightly cautions against certain moods and
hasty actions, but it does not provide specific guidance for
dealing with terrorism as a problem. There are many things
that can be done to curtail terrorist activities. Paul R. Pillar
has provided a helpful list, which includes (1) diplomacy,
(2) criminal law (referring to the legal process within the jurisdiction of the United States that can prosecute terrorist acts
within our borders), (3) financial controls, (4) military force,
(5) intelligence, and (6) covert action. This is a list of actions,
each of which has potential usefulness, but (as Pillar points
out) none of them can be regarded as a sole and sufficient
means to deal with the problem. The order is suggestive
because it begins with nonmilitary options. Doing that alone
offers a significant alternative to some of the ways being trumpeted as the really "serious" ways to deal with terrorism.[2]

Almost every one of the instruments listed by Pillar is
available to the government and shaped according to its policies. But this begs a question: Is government action the only
possible way to deal with terrorism? Is there no place for non-
governmental agencies that play important roles in countries
where human needs are great? Is there no place for communities of faith, especially those that are increasingly cognizant
of each other and often engaged in dialogue across international boundaries? Does the involvement of commercial
groups in global interchanges have no possible relevance to
this problem? Are cultural exchanges to be dismissed as
insignificant? Are the ways in which individual nations conduct their own internal affairs—particularly how such nations
treat the poor and the marginalized within their borders—of
no significance for how they are perceived in the wider
world? Is the task of countering terrorism to be confined only
to what governments can do through official policies, or is ter-

rorism something that can be ameliorated by working with people of other places through channels of interaction and mutual influence? What does globalization mean if it does not mean that individuals are somehow freed (at least in limited ways) from the iron cages of all controlling national loyalties and the psychic imprisonment of unquestioning forms of patriotic allegiance? Perhaps no more important contribution to thinking about ways to overcome terrorism is needed than to highlight the possibility of contributions that may come from an ever widening and increasingly important inter-change between peoples of the world interacting as people. Many persons with conservative leanings tend to downplay the importance of government in the conduct of affairs within the borders of the nation, yet these same conservatives often emphasize the importance of the military capacity of govern-ment when dealing with external affairs. Perhaps they might be helpful in pointing to the possibility that much can be done outside of the role of government in the international sphere as well as in domestic affairs.

This chapter is concerned less with discussing specific tools that can be used to deal with terrorism than identifying three models for putting those tools to use within the frame-work of a guiding agenda. Perhaps the most important issue facing the United States is which of these models will gov-ern its policies, or if more than one model is to be used, how they can be related to each other. The term "model" desig-nates an overall conceptual framework that governs the way or ways in which tools or strategies such as Pillar has listed are understood and employed. The model that is adopted is very crucial because all tools and strategies will be utilized or rejected, shaped and implemented, in order to conform to the model. That is why a debate about alternative models—a debate that has been relatively lacking as compared with the import of the issues—is so important. The impulse to do something, to do something really decisive and effective without considering all the ramifications, can prompt hasty actions that may even be countereffective.

War Intensified: The Crusade Model

The response that has been mounted by the United States against the threat of terrorism, especially as shaped by the administration, has been based on a model of warfare. This model is oriented primarily, if not exclusively, toward using military force as a means of stopping those who endanger our interests and security. Because terrorism is so scary, this response has tended to carry the idea of making "war" against terrorism to new heights. The impulse has been to rachet up the response to a great intensity. When faced with an unprecedented danger, it is natural to suppose that the fury of the response should be proportional to the threat, that the zeal with which a danger is opposed will make the effort resolute, and that the intensity with which the conflict is pursued will affect the completeness with which the danger can be eradicated. These impulses are typical of a crusade, according to which war must be conducted as vigorously as possible in order to erase evil. They significantly change the tendency of just war thinking toward restraint and limitation to the hallmarks of the crusade—rigor and completeness.

This crusading stance is often revealed as much or even more in the rhetoric used to talk about what is being done as in the specific actions that are undertaken. Such rhetoric has major consequences in the dynamics of international affairs because it shapes the perceptions that are formed about what is being attempted, perceptions created in the minds of those against whom the effort is directed and also in the minds of those who are friendly bystanders and potential allies. Even modest and prudent strategies may be given the appearance of truculence and domination when they are characterized with terminology that legitimizes them with the features of the crusade. Those who make the speeches that explain the policy, that cheer along the troops, or that satiate a public desire to have a quick and decisive solution to the problem of terrorism quite naturally find the terminology of the crusade more useful for their purposes than talk that refers to the struggle against terrorism as a serious yet limited effort to achieve a minimally necessary restraint on wrongdoing— that is, as a necessary obligation involving taking some actions that are very difficult, even morally painful.

One of the important contributions of Christian reflection about the Second World War was to develop the realization that war may be necessary but is never a satisfactory way to deal with evil. The stance of agonized participation significantly cancelled out the self-righteousness that had been associated with a morality of the crusade during the First World War. The resulting humility may well have made possible constructive peacemaking following the cessation of hostilities and done something to restrain the temptations to truculence that always attend superiority in conflict. Thinking based on the model of a crusade is impatient with such nuances. All sense of ambiguity, of the possibility that all parties have contributed to the conditions that make the problem so acute, and all considerations of how the crusader might need to change its own policies and goals to deal with the problem it seeks to solve are placed aside in the drive to overcome an enemy. Military action is seen as a righteous effort rather than a tragic necessity. Instead of being the means by which an enemy is forced to accept the conditions that make its membership in the world community tolerable, crusader thinking holds that quashing or annihilating the enemy is needed to overcome the problem.

Crusaders tend to be very suspicious of those who express concern about, sympathy with, or understanding of those whom they deem the adversary. They are suspicious of those who will not jump on the bandwagon. Crusaders expect everyone to rally to their side, to render support and encouragement unconditionally, to line up on the correct side of a sharply polarized contrast between good and evil. Yet, ironically, crusaders will often accept the aid and help of others in their cause even if those others do not share their own values and commitments. For instance, democracies will utilize the military power of dictatorships if that serves their purposes. The test becomes whether or not others will join the fray, not whether their political goals are compatible. However, if crusaders do not succeed in enlisting the support of others, they pursue their goals unilaterally.

Crusaders often act out of a sense of destiny. This may take the form of believing they are divinely appointed to subdue the evil they deplore. While the idea of the crusade is most obvious when it is conducted as a religious calling, crusades also arise from the feeling that a task is particularly crucial by virtue of the historical circumstances that have made it so important. This prompts crusaders to measure their obligations, not by considerations of prudence and pragmatic outcomes, but in terms of mandates and ultimate successes. They feel that they must eliminate a problem rather than bring it under reasonable control, save the world from evil rather than merely keep evil from disrupting the world.

The logic of the crusade model helps to explain developments that have occurred in the "war on terrorism." The first of these is the reconceptualizing of the fundamental role of defense planning as described by the office of the president in a document entitled *The National Security Strategy of the United States of America.*[3] This document explains and defends new policies for shaping America's role in the world. While it acknowledges the importance of international cooperation, the fundamental assumptions behind it are that of a nation called by destiny to use its strength to bear the burden of, and determine the overall strategy for, combating terrorism. In combating terrorism the document clearly states that the strategy will be conducted unilaterally if necessary and may well involve the use of preemptive strikes. This document affirms:

> We will disrupt and destroy terrorist organizations by:
>
> —direct and continuous action using all the elements of national and international power. Our immediate focus will be those terrorist organizations of global reach and any terrorist or state sponsor of terrorism which attempt to gain or use weapons of mass destruction (WMD) or their precursors;
>
> —defending the United States, the American people, and our interests at home and abroad by identifying and destroying the threat before it reaches our borders. While the United States will constantly strive to enlist the support of the international community, we will not hesitate to act alone, if necessary, to exercise our right of self-defense by acting preemptively against such terorists, to prevent them from doing harm against our people and our country; and
>
> —denying further sponsorship, support, and sanctuary to terrorists by convincing or compelling states to accept their sovereign responsibilities.[4]

This formulation about the goal of national security shifts the presumption about military action in a major way. Such action is to be used not merely as a way of responding to threats that seem unable to be stopped by other means (last resort), but as an instrument that is employed aggressively to stop evildoers before they can raise the threat to a dangerous level (preemptive strike). If it is wise and prudent to use force as soon as necessary to prevent malfeasance, then that action will become a version of aggression, not a form of defense. The military services were once administered by the "War Department." The title was changed many years ago to

"Defense Department." Perhaps this new policy means that the name should revert to its earlier form.

Despite some similarities, crusaders are not quite the same as realists. Realists believe in power as the necessary and only effective response to threats; crusaders believe in using power to prevent threats from becoming serious. There is a difference between deterrence and preemption. That conceptual contrast underlies this fundamental change in thinking about national security. The logic of the new defense policy, given the assumptions provided by the model of the crusade, is understandable. Strike before being struck, act before you or those for whom you have assumed responsibility are harmed. Many years ago, in the early stages of the Cold War, there was much talk of preventive war, of attacking those who were potential enemies before they could attack us. That talk was never turned into official policy nor acted upon, perhaps because just war thinking—however limited its influence—was the model that governed most thinking at the time. The model used was deterrence, not preemption. This new policy would probably not have resulted in the same restraint.

Crusaders tend to demonize enemies in order to have a clear idea of whom to attack. Because terrorism is so diffuse, it does not provide such a clear identity of who is the most direct cause of the danger. Who must be destroyed in order to create security? When using a crusade model, the natural tendency is to make nation-states the enemy, which is what happens in war. That may explain why military action was mounted against Afghanistan, which harbored Al Qaeda and groups associated with Al Qaeda, and may explain even more why Iraq, with its potential to aid terrorists with weapons of mass destruction, was invaded. But what will happen when individual nations are defeated and yet terrorism does not cease? Will we have to find other nations against which it is plausible to direct military action—so that preemptive strikes go on and on?

Terrorism and the crusading employment of force may actually exacerbate each other. Both contribute to the further reliance upon the use of force that became so much a part of life in the twentieth century and threatens to be even more alarming in the twenty-first century. Crusaders tend to function with the same premise as terrorists—that violence is the ultimate sanction for controlling human behavior. This can also be seen, for instance, in the use of surprise retaliation as a way of punishing terrorism, which assumes that the only way to counter violence is to possess a greater capacity for violence and to use it with deliberate resolve. Nothing in the crusade model promises to break the circle of violence. It merely pushes the circle of violence to higher and higher levels. The restraints that have been advocated and partially achieved in international conflict as a result of just war thinking will be set back seriously, perhaps even abandoned completely. The United States, a powerful nation feeling the warrant for exercising its power unilaterally if necessary, might even come to act in ways that actually conform to the image its detractors have of it. Moreover, the United States will bear the onus for the violence of retaliatory actions taken by those with whom it is allied. One does not have to be a pacifist to realize that the circle of violence is not brought to an end by the achievement of a superior level of violence by any one party. Although weak groups may be temporarily scared into ceasing to employ violence to achieve their objectives, they will nurse resentments and try again in the future to gain their way by threats. And since terrorism allows weak groups to employ violence even without having the massive capabilities of major military powers, they may not need to become the stronger party in order to pose a problem.

This is the model that the capabilities and the structures of world affairs make most available at the present time. Those who embrace it believe they are acting nobly, serving humanity, and keeping wrong from gaining the upper hand.

Their case can be appealing, especially if there are no alternatives to contemplate, or if the only alternatives are believed to be appeasement or surrender. But there are other models that ought to be considered—more exploratory, less familiar perhaps, and although less developed into plausible form possibly more promising and less likely to keep violence the major dynamic of public life.

Law Enforcement: One Alternative Model

To examine the limits and dangers of one model does not by itself constitute a responsible response to terrorism. To propose alternatives, difficult as that may be, is required of those who seek to be faithful. Perhaps there are institutions and aspects of the international social process that can be utilized to create different models for counterterrorist activity. The development of constitutionally governed law enforcement may be the very achievement of free societies that is most worthy of being commended to the world as a whole. It is unfortunate its value and importance is often overlooked when people embark on crusades. The model of law enforcement is worth considering—not law enforcement as a form of social control within just one jurisdiction, but law enforcement as a model of international cooperation created to bring all nations together into a common effort to repudiate terrorism and to regard it as criminal activity against the whole of humanity. Such a model would take the threat of terrorism seriously, so seriously, in fact, as to realize it cannot be eliminated by compulsive actions or unilaterally executed coercion, however well intentioned, however massive.

Terrorism is largely the work of small, dedicated, unauthorized or covertly acting individuals (or relatively small functional units). The scope and contours of terrorism cut across all national boundaries. The world is not clearly divided between terrorist states and nonterrorist states (though admittedly some regimes and some nations are more willing to support or employ terrorism than others). Instead, terrorism can threaten every nation and be aimed against any nation by groups working from any base. Countries can be threatened by terrorist activity even from within, either from their own citizens or from others. In this respect, the threat it poses resembles criminal activity more than warfare.

Admittedly, the law enforcement model is not presently well developed on an international scale. To proceed along the lines of this model would require an imaginative extension of international law and a high degree of cooperation between all nations. It would probably transcend autonomous national sovereignty even further than does humanitarian intervention—but for similarly legitimate reasons. It would require the overwhelming majority of nations to agree that the practice of violence along terrorist lines is a major problem for the world as a whole—that the consequences of tolerating, harboring, or utilizing unannounced, unpredictable, and randomly applied violence pose such a hazard to the well-being of all peoples that a concerted effort to repudiate and counteract such behavior is one of the most important agendas in our time. Opposing terrorism this way would become a significant aspect of globalization, bringing all peoples of the world into a common effort to confront a common danger.

Some aspects of this model may already be at work. Nations are already employing investigative techniques in order to identify and apprehend terrorists who can be found within their borders. Such work is usually quiet, unheralded until successful, and depends more upon astuteness than heroics. It requires effective intelligence, which could become the global equivalent of skillful detective work. This model may also involve cooperation between the law enforcement agencies of several nations—to a degree that might not have been contemplated before terrorism called for it. Such cooperation

should aim toward internationally conducted trials and punishment. The international significance of such efforts would
overcome the problem created by one nation taking upon
itself the task of judging the guilt or innocence of persons who
belong to other nations.

The International Criminal Court, which came into being
in 2002, is an effort to institutionalize this model. It has been
designed to be an instrument for upholding the idea that the
citizens of various nations can be held responsible for crimes
against humanity, crimes of war and genocide, even if their
own governments have approved of what was done. Some
nations, most notably the United States, have resisted the
establishment of such a court because they fear it might
someday be used to judge as unacceptable the behavior of
officials carrying out the policies of their own governments
or peacekeeping duties under the auspices of the United
Nations. But courts are the very places where the determination of what constitutes a crime should be decided. It is not
good to put the determination of what is justice in the hands
of lone rangers from any nation, especially when they are
embarked on crusades.

Another embryonic form of policing on the international
level can be found in the use of inspectors in places that may
be arming with weapons of mass destruction. It is difficult
to show why it is improper to develop such weapons when
the major powers have them and refuse to give them up.
However, when in the judgment of the world community, the
further development of such weapons by a particular nation
is unacceptable, the use of inspectors to determine what is
being done and to counter the possibility of their further
development and use is a strategy consistent with the model
of policing. Like policing, it does not evaporate the problem;
however, it may aid in controlling it.

Admittedly, law enforcement is not free of potential problems. Police work can be corrupted and may be even more

difficult to keep under control than the behavior of armies. Law enforcement can be a source of oppression as well as an instrument of protection. It requires a highly developed professional competence and dedication to make it just and fair. It must be supported by a judicial system that is as concerned to protect the innocent as to condemn the guilty, to see that police behave and do not exercise their power without restraint. These requirements are not easily met, and are not adequately achieved in many nations at the present time. But such restraints are one of the unique marks of free societies. Much work would be required to extend them into wide use on an international scale, but to do so would be a challenge far more profound and far more likely to extend human well-being than to escalate the use of violence.

There is another premise behind the law enforcement model that must be recognized. Law enforcement does not eliminate criminal activity. It brings it under control so that life can go on with reasonable dispatch and viability. Many scholars of terrorism tell us that it will not be quickly overcome, that we can expect to live with it for some indefinite time. As Paul R. Pillar puts it, terrorism is a problem to be managed, but one that will never be solved.

> The long history of terrorism is reason enough to expect that it will always be a problem and usually a significant one. It is the product of such basic facts of human existence as the discontent that is sometimes strong enough to impel people toward violence, and the asymmetries of the weak confronting the strong, and the vulnerability of almost every facet of civilization to physical harm at the hands of those who find a reason to inflict harm. If there is a "war" against terrorism, it is a war that cannot be won.
>
> Counterterrorism, even though it shares some attributes with warfare, is not accurately represented by the metaphor of a war. Unlike most wars, it has neither a fixed set of enemies nor the prospect of coming to closure, be it through

a "win" or some other kind of denouement. Like the cold war, it requires long, patient, persistent effort, but unlike it, it will never conclude with the internal collapse of an opponent. There will be victories and defeats, but not big, tide-turning victories. Counterterrorism is a fight and a struggle, but it is not a campaign with a beginning and an end.[5]

It makes a difference whether one thinks a threat has to be eradicated (as in the crusade model) or simply held to tolerable limits (as in the law enforcement model). Both may employ the same strategies or tools, but with quite different goals in mind. One seeks the total subjugation, even the destruction, of the enemy; the other, the containment of the threat. The disagreements between those would embrace crusades and those who would prefer the criminal justice approach is very deep. One sees military power to be a means of crushing dangers; the other sees military power, if useful at all, as a means of keeping threats from becoming too great. This difference does not get resolved by logical argument or empirical considerations because the model functions as an ideology that makes all discussions of strategic usefulness into inconclusive clashes between incompatible political faith systems.

Adopting a different model for dealing with terrorism might also change the manner in which the United States would act in the exercise of its preeminence. It could change the image from that of an overbearing power to that of cooperative servant. Police work can be thought of as a form of servanthood rather than of mastery. It uses restrained power for the protection of the common good. Most empires have flaunted their capacity to make others conform to their wishes regardless of what those others feel is wise. Can the exercise of leadership from a position of overwhelming strength be carried out in ways that change that pattern, or will the position of empire remained inextricably mixed with the morality of the crusade?

Peacemaking: A Transformative Model

The model that will now be examined may seem to many so idealistic that nobody in their sober moments would put any stock in it. Perhaps this is the point for fools to enter. But a holy type of foolishness is often commended in Christian thinking and sometimes is the only stance from which evil is ever redeemed. It may be foolish to dismiss foolishness without at least letting it state its case. After all, there are different kinds of foolishness, including the foolishness of the world that drives itself toward disaster under the banner of being realistic.

This third model makes the bold assumption that it is possible to make peace even with those with whom there is disagreement, even with those who are antagonistic and presently driven by hate, and even with those whose behavior has taken violent forms. This model differs completely from that of the crusade, which has no place for even the slightest interaction with foes. It also differs from both just war thinking (which aims to limit and control the use of violence employed as a last resort) and pacifism (as the refusal to use violence.) Although both just war thinking and pacifism are alternatives to the crusade, they are still moral responses to war. The uniqueness of this model is that instead of responding to war as a moral problem it seeks to take an active initiative in order to achieve peace.

This transformative model is most fully developed in a body of thought that goes under the rubric "just peacemaking." The clue to just peacemaking, as it has been extensively developed by Glen Stassen, is a serious reading of the Sermon on the Mount as practical admonition to take reconciling initiatives to overcome the hostility of enemies.

The Sermon on the Mount is not about human striving toward high ideals but about God's transforming initiatives to deliver us from the vicious cycles in which we get stuck. It has a realistic view of our world, characterized by murder, anger, divorce, adultery, lust, deceit, enmity, hypocrisy, false prophets, and houses destined for destruction. It announces that in the midst of such bondage, there is also another force operating. God is also beginning to rule with justice and peace. . . . The Sermon on the Mount describes specific ways we can participate in the new initiatives God is taking.[6]

In the book in which he first proposed this idea Stassen offers seven steps for just peacemaking: (1) affirm common security interests with adversaries; (2) take independent initiatives; (3) talk with your enemy; (4) seek human rights and justice; (5) acknowledge vicious cycles; (6) end judgmental propaganda and make amends; and (7) work with citizens' groups for the truth. Every one of these steps is a way of creating dialogue aimed at healing conflict.

A subsequent study by a group of scholars building on the seven steps suggested by Stassen resulted in a book outlining ten practices for just peacemaking.[7] The principles developed in this book are not entirely new. What is significant about the study that came out of this group is the consensus it represents of thinking being done by people of somewhat different views and competencies: ethicists, biblical and moral theologians, scholars of international relations, peace activists, and practitioners of conflict resolution. Their work offers an alternative to the moral thinking that focuses only on the question whether or not war is justified and, if so, under what conditions. Instead, it directs attention to ways of dealing with conflicts without going to war or using the threat to do so as the bargaining chip.

Strategies commended by this group include the use of nonviolent direct action, taking independent initiatives to reduce threats, and utilizing various techniques of conflict resolution. Those who acknowledge their part in the creation of conflict and their part in patterns of injustice are far more willing to explore peacemaking as a possibility than those who view themselves as paragons of exemplary righteousness. Peacemaking involves concern for democracy, for human rights, and for religious liberty, as well as for just and sustainable worldwide economic development. Peacemaking need not be confined to what governments can do, though governments are important and the work of the United Nations especially important. If weaponry and the weapons trade are reduced, it will help to create a situation conducive to the implementation of peacemaking practices.

Stassen has subsequently taken the practices developed in the book and suggested how they are useful for taking actions to prevent terrorism. The details of his analysis are important, but the model he proposes is of even greater importance. Stassen asks:

> Is it time to turn to a deeper analysis of the roots of terrorism and terrorist recruitment? To be effective in combating terrorism and achieving better security, do we need something more than attacks on known terrorists and potential terrorists and financial pressure? Is it time to begin discussing initiatives that can decrease the resentment and anger that drive people to turn to terrorism? Is it time to turn to just peacemaking theory for help in suggesting preventive initiatives?[8]

The kind of thinking referred to above does not stand all by itself. There is a considerable interest in many places in finding ways to settle disputes without armed conflict. The Carter Center in Atlanta regularly pursues such possibilities. The United States Institute of Peace has studied the possibilities of using nonviolent strategies for overturning oppressive regimes. A recent report declares:

> There is need for a fuller appreciation within governments, international organizations, and the news media of

the dynamics and potential of strategic nonviolent conflict. An understanding of how these methods work and how nonviolent movements operate improves the ability of the international community to assist effectively and to incorporate them into global efforts to promote democracy.[9]

It is simply wrong to assume that there are no ways to deal with problems such as terrorism other than warfare and diplomatic efforts premised on the intention to use force if necessary. Just peacemaking is a sober elaboration of the possibilities in dialogue and negotiation. It sees these as useful, but not merely in the superficial sense of continued chatter between two sides that exchange views for awhile but know very well they will never come to agreement. Peacemaking is prepared to take risks because it is morally committed to bringing the sides together. It is not appeasement in the sense of bargaining to see what concessions will cause terrorists to back off; rather, it is exploration in the effort to see what common grounds furnish the possibility of transforming behavior. It is willingness to hear the terrorists and to learn what they are trying to say. In the first chapter we asked whether or not terrorism was a pathology. In therapy, listening to the disturbed is the entree to their healing, whereas oppressive measures only aggravate their feeling of estrangement. Is there any chance that could also be the case with terrorists?

These three models suggest very different ways of trying to deal with terrorism. They also hint at why the discussion about how to deal with terrorism is so difficult. Even a great amount of rational discussion seems to do little to nudge people out of thinking governed by one model into thinking governed by another. But the analysis of how these models work to govern strategies and practices may help people to understand how deeply they are controlled by the model to which they are committed. The starting ground is really something of a faith decision—whether or not it is identified as religiously grounded. Faiths sometimes change, not because their premises are refuted intellectually, but because some momentous trauma proves them inadequate. It is still to be seen whether the threat of terrorism will only further encase the world in its reliance on violence as the ultimate form of human interaction or if terrorism is sufficiently traumatic to provide the impetus for humankind to abandon reliance upon violence as an inadequate "faith."

Chapter 4

Terrorism and the Erosion
of Civil and Political Liberties

*T*he greatest danger terrorism poses may not be the deaths and destruction that come from physical attacks (the horror of which should not be forgotten or minimized), but the changes in the attitudes and practices of entire societies that lay aside safeguards of freedom in order to counteract terrorism's dangers. While terrorists can destroy infrastructures that they target without prior warning, such destruction will probably never be so widespread as to render a country inoperative or to destroy it totally. But the fear terrorists can create even by small-scale actions may affect the mood of an entire society and bring about momentous changes in the willingness of that society to sustain the risks that are necessary in order to be free. A society that seeks to be completely protected against the danger of terrorism is very likely to undercut its freedoms in ways that adversely affect all its citizens. A fortress society cannot be created without becoming a police state.

Although in some respects these considerations take the argument about how to deal with terrorism in a somewhat different direction, these are issues that cannot be ignored. The preservation of domestic liberties and concern for human rights in the world at large must remain central concerns. Such concerns can be rendered peripheral when attention focuses only on how terrorism can be effectively countered, especially when the model for doing so emphasizes the repressive use of force. But if the very procedures and safeguards that protect liberty and enhance human rights are either deliberatively curtailed or simply laid aside in the struggle against the terrorist threat, there is a sense in which it may be said that terrorism has conquered us rather than we have overcome terrorism.

No matter which model is used to counter terrorism, threats will continue to be present to the internal life of every nation—not least in those nations that cherish freedom and seek to keep governments from imposing excessive restrictions on individual liberties. Liberties are difficult to maintain without the societal openness the terrorists can exploit to their advantage. Those who bear responsibilities for public security must be concerned about the threats terrorism poses to the health and safety of the citizenry. Their work is obviously more difficult in societies that respect and honor civil liberties than in societies that are accustomed to tight controls. No society can be completely safe from attack and free at the same time.

Officials who are responsible for public safety not infrequently chafe under the constitutional provisions that limit their power to act, and when they face new or unusual threats they quite understandably plead the need for additional powers to take actions to ensure the public's safety. From one perspective, that is their calling; from another, it becomes the scenario by which free societies let their own most valuable features be curtailed.

Somewhat Easier Issues

In dealing with the tension between achieving security and maintaining freedoms, it helps to draw some distinction between various dangers and to differentiate the dangers to liberty in the possible responses. These are not always the same in every case. There are, for instance, security measures that are relatively benign with respect to civil liberties. They are more likely to create inconvenience than oppression. For example, passenger screening at airports and attendee screening at public events, which are designed to prevent individuals from taking along items that could be put to dangerous use, pose relatively little threat to civil liberties. The right to possess arms in places where such arms can be used to create havoc is not crucial for civil liberty. Hence, to prohibit the possession of guns, knives, and other means of inflicting harm by persons using planes, trains, buses, or attending schools or public events is an acceptable restriction on behavior. Of course, we may have reason to regret these inconveniences and to feel uneasy when being subjected to them. But the need to prevent violence from occurring in public places will be with us for a long time, and the measures seeking to do so are designed to protect our safety.

But even these relatively benign measures to protect the public safety must be constantly reviewed lest they slowly change into discriminatory practices. Such measures should be applied across the board to all persons who wish to participate in the public activities in question. The screening that takes place to prevent the possession of dangerous devices in vulnerable places should be done to all persons without regard to their ethnic identity, economic or social status, political outlooks, or religious beliefs. Any special screening that is done should be determined by random selection, not by so-called profiling. There are bound to be pressures to streamline these measures. For instance, there is currently a proposal to flag every airline reservation as it is made with a category: "clear," "scrutinize," or "deny." Such designations would be determined by asking questions about age, birthplace, background, address, even credit card record and the like (hopefully not what one writes in books or says from platforms!). Those individuals placed into the "scrutinize" category would be further examined at the gate, and those in the "deny" category turned away. Although possibly advantageous to those who are designated "clear," since it would speed their boarding flights, this proposal has many possibilities for becoming a means of discrimination—denying a civil liberty such as the right to fly on public carriers—without people knowing why the right is being denied or being able to challenge the category imposed. To be caught carrying a knife or gun hidden in carry-on baggage is one thing—the threat has been made clearly apparent. Failing a set of queries by a reservations clerk or security agent is another; that could very well deprive a privilege without adequate cause.

Closing certain streets or airspaces to general public access would be another inconvenient but possibly benign way of enhancing security. If the alert level reaches orange or red, there is a plan to close certain harbor areas to most uses—barring pleasure boats and possibly fishing vessels. Such measures can take away a civil liberty a bit more than security screening at airports because they would deny a privilege on a wholesale or blanket basis by stopping an activity rather than seeking to monitor it for misuse. Instead of searching vessels to see whether or not they are friendly and benign, it would simply stop the use of the waterways, at least temporarily. There may be reasons for taking measures of this sort, particularly in areas that are especially vulnerable. But all such measures—whether on land or sea—must be fully scrutinized so they are not configured in ways that adversely affect certain groups more than others. Closing certain streets or certain areas, for example, could be used to prevent demonstrators from mounting protests in locations where such witness would have a significant visibility. That could be done to hamper the free expression of ideas as much as to protect crucial installations. It might not be entirely clear in every instance which of these motives controlled the decision making of authorities.

But actions taken by governmental authorities are not the only possible threat to civil liberties. On March 3, 2003, an incident took place in a shopping mall in upstate New York that sent chilling signals around the country. A lawyer of good standing was wearing a T-shirt that he had just purchased within the mall with the wording "Give Peace a Chance." He was approached by two security guards, who ordered him to take off the shirt or leave the mall. He refused to do either and was subsequently arrested at the behest of the mall owners by the police of the jurisdiction in which the mall is located. He was charged with trespassing—"knowingly entering or remaining unlawfully on the premises." We do not know what wording was on the T-shirts of others in the mall at the time, though it is difficult to suppose that all the T-shirts were blank. Nor can we be sure the security guards would have asked a person wearing a slogan such as "Attack the Tyrant Now" to leave. Although the charges in this case have been dropped, since they had to be pressed by the owners of the mall for the case to go forward, this is a disturbing event. It raises important questions about the right of private property owners who engage in commercial activities serving the public to control the expression of opinion on their premises The security guards in this case told the T-shirt wearer this was "like a private house and that he was acting poorly." That explanation is inconsistent with the spirit of the innkeepers' principle that those who offer public services cannot use arbitrary criteria to exclude access to their services. It would be a serious blow to societal openness if people were forced to hide their views or throttle their convictions in order to make use of important and necessary privately owned commercial services.

There may be important reasons to exercise voluntary discretion in discussing issues infused with wartime emotions. This is not to advocate silence for the sake of harmony, but caution for the sake of dialogue. This is a matter that has to be handled skillfully in every group of which we are a part.

In churches, for example, every preacher must wrestle with the tension between prophetic utterance and pastoral concern, between moral leadership and institutional viability. The sermon is often a form of one-way conversation that can become an instrument of power. How a preacher deals with this possibility is a very sensitive matter and cannot be decided apart from the dynamics of the local context. Some preachers will decide to put on T-shirts in the pulpit—some of which will say, "Give Peace a Chance," and others, "Attack the Tyrant Now." A few local congregations will be composed entirely of those who favor one slogan; a few congregations, of those who favor the other. But how much is gained from preaching one position to a congregation already in agreement? Most congregations will be composed of persons holding different views with great tenacity and vehemence. What is the role of preaching in those situations—which often tempt silence and avoidance? Clearly it is important to acknowledge the difference of opinion and to indicate how this reveals the limitations of moral judgments in a human condition of finitude and sin. It is also legitimate, indeed helpful, to explore the ramifications of different positions, a task that can be enriched by examining stands taken by denominational and ecumenical bodies. Last, it is legitimate to make one's own position known. The pulpit can be misused, however, if it demands consent to the particular views of an individual in a way that implies a failure to do so is a breach of fidelity.

In a healthy church these matters will not be treated only from the pulpit. They will be open for discussion, at a minimum, in "feedback" opportunities during or after the service. They should be matters for study in adult sessions that focus on public issues from the perspective of faith, that look carefully at what serious thinkers are offering in the way of guidance and insight about particular issues. In the church, this will include looking at what theologians and ethicists are saying as well as the social witness output of denominations.

A similar dynamic should be cherished in the larger arenas of public life. The confrontation with terrorism will undoubtedly produce sharp disagreements about matters on which feelings run high. This possibility requires us to pay special attention to the art of respectful disagreement. That is an important aspect of living within a democratic society and crucial to having informed debate about issues that need to be resolved through corporate decision making. The democratic process can be seriously harmed if the fear that terrorism breeds leads to polarizations that make dialogue difficult, if not impossible. Although, strictly speaking, this is not viewed as a matter of civil liberty, it is a matter of civic health. The ideal of freedom of expression often gets lip service more readily than it is fully and effectively practiced, especially under the kind of duress the threat of terrorism can create.

More Difficult Issues

After any terrorist attack there is bound to be widespread apprehension among members of the general public with respect to their safety, even though the statistical likelihood of being the victim of a terrorist attack is not high. The possible use of chemical and biological weapons might change the statistical probabilities, but that would not necessarily significantly raise the apprehension. The element of unpredictability, the sense of having one's "space" violated, and the experience of vulnerability when pursuing the ordinary affairs of life prompt both fear and anger. The natural impulse is to demand that measures be taken to see that events such as those already experienced do not happen again—that every possible means be used to make the future secure.

Every terrorist attack on the United States has been followed by the enactment of new "antiterrorist" legislation. Such legislation does not change the status of the violent acts which terrorists do; these are already crimes under existing laws and already carry penalties to deter people from doing them. What most so-called "anti-terrorist" legislation does is to weaken or remove restrictions on the policing power of government—restrictions that are the hard-won provisions of constitutional law developed over many years in order to protect citizens from the arbitrary use of governmental power. Recently, legislation designed to make counterterrorist measures easier to take has been passed in response to terrorism during both a Democratic and a Republican administration—under the tutelage of both liberal and conservative attorney generals. Each of the major terrorist attacks on the United States—that on the World Trade Center on February 26, 1993; that on the Murrah Federal Building in Oklahoma City on April 19, 1995; that at the Olympic Games in Atlanta in 1996; and those on the World Trade Center and Pentagon on September 11, 2001—has been followed by legislation increasing the investigative and policing powers of the federal government. As these laws have been signed, the president at the time has declared that the necessary provisions to prevent terrorists from carrying out their destructive purposes have now been put into place. But the attacks do not completely stop. The result has been a cycle of attack, antiterrorist legislation, another attack, more antiterrorist legislation, and so forth. This response pattern is not a comforting one for civil liberties.

The most important piece of antiterrorist legislation is one designated by this long title: "Uniting and Strengthening America by Providing Appropriate Tools Required to Intercept and Obstruct Terrorism Act of 2001." Known popularly as the "Patriot Act," this legislation provides, among other things, for the secret detention of aliens simply if they are deemed dangerous, for the designation of organizations as terrorist on the basis of undisclosed evidence without a hearing and without making that designation public, and for the expansion of government authority for search and surveillance of groups that are deemed suspicious.

The threats to civil liberty that this legislation poses have been pointed out by a number of concerned groups and individuals. Interestingly enough, indeed very significantly, some of the sharpest criticism has come from political conservatives (on the so-called right), as well as from respected scholars in the middle. Criticism from such sources is less easy to dismiss as alarmist than shrill warnings coming from more radical groups at demonstrations. The fear that civil liberties are threatened is not entirely far-fetched, and the sleepy assurance of many people that all is well with American freedom could be the greatest danger of all. For example, here is how one think tank that would generally be considered conservative describes the danger:

> Government officials typically respond to terrorist attacks by proposing and enacting "antiterrorism" legislation. To assuage the widespread anxiety of the populace, policymakers make the dubious claim that they can prevent terrorism by curtailing the privacy and civil liberties of the people. Because everyone wants to be safe and secure, such legislation is usually very popular and passes the legislative chambers of Congress with lopsided majorities. As the president signs the antiterrorism bill into effect, too many people indulge in the assumption that they are now safe, since the police with their newly acquired powers, will somehow be able to foil the terrorism before they can kill again. The plain truth, however, is that it is only a matter of time before the next attack.
>
> This cycle of terrorist attack followed by government curtailment of civil liberties must be broken—or our society will eventually lose the key attribute than has made it great—freedom.[1]

Police surveillance has frequently been used allegedly in an effort to monitor possible sources of trouble on the presumption that such activities are needed in order to protect the public. But the record on this matter indicates that it is frequently used not to discover dangers, but to identify opponents of government policy. Even groups like Amnesty International and the American Friends Service Committee have been targeted for infiltration on the premise they might cause disruptions. Individuals who engage in political activity—especially those who oppose current policies—have had files created detailing their controversial stands. Such surveillance was practiced during the struggle for civil rights even against groups clearly committed to nonviolence, and it was prevalent during certain periods of the Cold War. This practice can have a chilling effect on the advocacy of alternative policies—the very advocacy that is so essential to wise and informed debates about issues that are in need of examination. Moreover, files on individuals can be used as instruments of repression if constitutional protections are eroded or set aside. These dangerous practices increase during times of stress and disagreement. Terrorism could well become the excuse for doing more and more of this.

I recall having been taken aback when someone at a professional meeting I was attending alarmingly declared that the United States is on the road to becoming like Nazi Germany. But later I read the following passage from a scholarly paper written by David Little, whom I respect for fair and balanced judgments. The paper considers the process by which appeals to public emergency were used by Hitler to secure his grasp of power. It makes this observation:

> When a nation is mortally threatened by enemies within and without as Hitler believed Germany to be in the early 30s, the nation's only recourse, he thought, is to turn to the old adage, "necessity knows no law." Consequently article 48 [the emergency article of the Weimar Constitution allowing for suspension of civil liberties] conformed perfectly to his

basic philosophy, which was, in effect, that anything and everything is justified when the life of the nation is at fundamental risk.[2]

Little goes on to note that the charter of the United Nations calls for respecting human rights. The subsequent development of international law and the supporting institutional practices that have been developed through the efforts of the United Nations "were designed to redefine forever the permissible limits of, and reasons for, the use of force, so that what Hitler had wrought in the mid-twentieth century, or anything close to it, might never occur again."[3]

There has been much concern for human rights ever since the end of the Second World War, much of it connected with the work of the United Nations. Although the charter makes references to human rights, the enunciation of basic principles is found in the Universal Declaration of Human Rights adopted by the General Assembly in 1948. That action was followed in 1966 and 1976 by two other documents that further explicate principles for protecting human rights. One of these, the International Covenant on Civil and Political Rights, contains an emergency clause allowing states to deal with threats to their well-being that are out of the ordinary. Among the provisions in article 4 we find these stipulations:

> 1) In times of public emergency which threatens the life of a nation and the existence of which is officially proclaimed, the States Parties to the present Covenant may take measures derogating from their obligations under the present Covenant to the extent strictly required by the exigencies of the situation, provided that such measures are not inconsistent with their other obligations under international law and do not involve discrimination solely on the grounds of race, color, language, religion, or social origin.

2) No derogation [among others] from articles 6 [prohibition of arbitrary life-taking], 7 [prohibition of the use of torture, cruel, unusual or degrading treatment or punishment], 8 [prohibition of enslavement], and 18 [protection of freedom of thought, conscience, religion or belief] may be made under this provision.

A third paragraph of this document provides that any State Party to the Covenant availing itself of derogation shall immediately inform the other States Parties of that action through the secretary general of the United Nations. According to Little, this article "was formulated to require *public accountability, full disclosure,* and *the observance of basic standards of human decency* in the face of public emergency."[4]

The development of terrorism creates enormous pressures to move in ways that undercut the foregoing provisions and could even threaten to reverse or undo the concern about human rights that has been among the important concerns of the international community in recent decades. Reasons of state may come into conflict with humanitarian concerns in ways that startle idealism and shatter confidence in the power of free institutions to protect themselves. For instance, Alan Dershowitz, whose commitment to human rights has been highly visible throughout his entire career, attracted a good deal of "sound bite" attention with a chapter of a book in which he contended that torture might be warranted if used against terrorists to obtain information about planned actions that would take the lives of innocent people.

The simple cost-benefit analysis for employing such nonlethal torture seems overwhelming: it is surely better to inflict nonlethal pain on one guilty terrorist who is illegally withholding information needed to prevent an act of terrorism than to permit a large number of innocent victims to die. Pain is a lesser and more remediable harm than death;

and the lives of a thousand innocent people should be val-
ued more than the bodily integrity of one guilty person.[5]

It is important to understand Dershowitz's position cor-
rectly. He is not advocating that we begin to use torture for
the first time. He cites persuasive evidence that almost all
countries are already using nonlethal torture to obtain information from terrorists—"off the books and under the radar
screen." What he proposes is to set up a provision for using
torture under judicial supervision—under warrants similar to
those currently required to conduct searches of private property. If torture will be used anyway, those doing so while the
law totally forbids it are placed in a difficult position and are
even likely to go to excesses they would avoid if under judicial supervision. The democratic process would be better
protected, argues Dershowitz, under his proposal to oversee
it by judicial requirements than it is under the present situation, in which torture is used but without being acknowledged or supervised.

This line of reasoning illustrates how great a pressure terrorism creates to suspend or to abandon humanitarian concerns in order to cope with the dangers it poses. If the logic
for using torture is convincing even to those with a commendable history of concern for human rights, how much
more convincing it will be for those who are inclined to
emphasize safety and reasons of state as overriding factors.

Those who administer justice and bear the responsibility
for protecting the safety of citizens are often tempted to over-
step their authority. A long investigative report contending
that they did so in the case of John Walker Lindh was carried
in the *New Yorker*.[6] Written after the clamor about the case
had settled down and the list of charges against Walker was
reduced from ten counts to one, this piece of investigative
reporting shows how easily the emotions created by terrorism can derail concern for fairness and due process in the

administration of criminal justice. John Walker Lindh, the young American whose youthful exploration with Muslim teachings led him into involvement with the Taliban, became an object of Justice Department scorn as a person who had provided aid and comfort to America's enemies. The charges initially placed against him would have brought three life sentences plus an additional ninety years in prison. Lindh was considered an enemy of the state, prohibited from speaking to the media, apparently denied legal counsel, and otherwise kept under special confinement—aspects of which were essentially punitive. The author of the article indicates that much of this happened in the immediate aftermath of September 11, when feelings were high and knowledge about Islam, terrorism, and related matters was relatively unsophisticated. Much attention has subsequently been given to this individual and the activities in which he engaged—sometimes at great danger and discomfort to himself. Experts who interviewed him concluded he was not a determined terrorist, as the Justice Department assumed when his association with Al Qaeda came to light, but a misguided kid who fell into disturbing circumstances.

The article indicates the measures taken by the Justice Department and other federal agencies to make their case stick, including threats against law enforcement officials who attempted to provide Lindh with the protections of the American legal system to which as a citizen he was entitled. The Lindh case is an example of how "reasons of state" can threaten civil liberties in time of national emergency. The legal system eventually prevented this case from becoming as serious a blot on the record of American jurisprudence as it seemed headed to be, though by dropping most of the charges the Justice Department has been able to obscure from public attention the dangers in some of its initial actions. Originally, the Justice Department apparently wanted to make an example of Lindh, perhaps to send a message to any persons tempted to follow his wanderings that they would be treated harshly. But think what a different approach to this case could have done. Instead of making the point that the United States will make an example of waywardness by visiting it with intense retribution, a different handling of the case could have made an example of the United States as a nation with a compassionate soul, one that can recognize wrongdoing without having to visit it with maximum vindictiveness. In the process of seeking to be appreciated by the world at large, that might have been a very persuasive gesture and it might have done more to reduce the impulses that breed terrorism than meeting out maximum punishment would have.

Reasons of state often undercut other cherished safeguards of due process that are essential to democratic society. The handling of the prisoners who have been captured in the military action against terrorism in Afghanistan and sent to the U.S. naval base in Guantanamo, Cuba, has been devised in part to keep them from meeting with lawyers. On March 11, 2003, an appellate court upheld this procedure on the ground that these detainees are not Americans and are not housed within the borders of the United States. They are not therefore entitled to the safeguards offered citizens by the Constitution. There may be some strategic reasons (that is, reasons of state exercised for emergency purposes) for treating these detainees in ways that do not conform to the international protocol for the treatment of prisoners of war and/or to deny them the due process that American law is supposed to offer to accused persons (at least to citizens), but what message does this send to the world? When claiming that the war against Iraq is a war to extend democracy to a nation that has suffered under brutal tyranny, how is the case made more plausible by suspending some of the most important aspects of democratic ways of dealing with wrongdoing on the part of those who run afoul of American power? Apparently those who have great power are not obliged to commend their actions to others but can act as they wish and harbor the comforting illusion that everybody will want to feel their way of life is something to be sought after even if in combating terrorism they seek to suspend the very safeguards that are the distinguishing features of democratic societies.

To be sure, there are important safeguards left in American law. Among them is the freedom of press and pulpit as well as academic professionals to bring critical analysis of these matters to the attention of the public. But if the public does not respond, does not see the issues or care enough to safeguard the very constitutional and procedural safeguards that keep a society from becoming oppressive, what is the profit from their prophetic diligence? If terrorism scares us so much as to make us afraid of being free, the outcome could be as much a disaster as if much of the physical property we have were to be destroyed. The cherished cry "Give me liberty or give me death" should not be replaced with the phrase "Erode my liberty to prevent my death."

Chapter 5

Religion, Morality, and Terrorism

*T*he several different perspectives on, and models for dealing with, terrorism have deep roots in fundamental commitments—commitments that are religious in nature even if not always in name. If anything, terrorism has shown how deeply religion still influences human behavior whether for good or ill. It makes us keenly aware that scientific and secular thinking have not replaced faith commitments and religious motivations—not even in those cultures most shaped by the secularizing tendencies of the Enlightenment. This chapter will examine how religious faith and religiously based moral outlooks are related to the different ways of responding to the threat terrorism poses.

As we have seen, there are deep differences in thinking about the nature and causes of terrorism and in the proposals suggested for dealing with it. Examining these differences from the perspective of religion is not likely to produce agreement over which of the alternatives is strategically feasible or morally correct. The religious factor often intensifies rather than overcomes the disagreements that persist about all political and social judgments. Religion seldom, if ever, provides answers or solutions to questions that are unresolved on other grounds.

But examining such matters through the lens of religion can help to clarify the guiding premises behind them. Even if the role played by religion in relation to different responses to terrorism does not settle issues between different positions, this does not mean there is no benefit to be had from describing those differences and showing how they arise out of deeper contrasts in thinking about the ultimate nature and purpose of human existence. This process can be helpful because it advances the understanding of the problem even if it does not solve it. Moreover, to understand the deeper currents of meaning and commitments that lie behind moral differences can also help to provide resources for living with dilemmas without being overwhelmed by despair. No attempt at describing these matters is likely to enjoy universal approval. Every person stands in a unique position that shapes the task itself and affects the outcome of the effort. There are bound to be persistent differences in identifying the religious stances that are involved, but this does not mean that the descriptive task is entirely controlled by prior faith-commitments or completely short-circuited by the inevitability of individual perspectives. Some helpful insights are possible. Some writers do better than others at being analytical without being polemical. Journalists are frequently as successful as professors (and often clearer). Although the distinction between descriptive fairness and partisan advocacy is never altogether complete, that difference is worth attempting to observe in the effort to sort out the issues and to appreciate more fully the interconnectedness between religious faith and political behavior.

Assumptions behind the Peacemaking Model

We begin by looking at the faith convictions behind the just peacemaking model because these are frequently stated explicitly and are in most cases central to the embrace of this approach. Many of those who advocate this model acknowledge their reliance upon faith as a source of moral guidance, their indebtedness to ideas and ideals that derive from a religious heritage, and their allegiance to the traditions of a believing community. In the case of others who embrace this view, the acknowledgment is less explicit but is nevertheless discernible.[1]

Those for whom peacemaking seems promising believe that human beings are capable of living and acting together, of identifying and resolving (or at least mitigating) the differences that cause disputes. They take the position that no nation (and no group and no individual) is so incapable of change of life as to make its annihilation the only possible way to deal with a matter about which there is controversy. This conviction is grounded in a confidence that there is a latent commitment to goodwill in human beings that transcends particular creedal specifics and that has not been entirely snuffed out even in the seemingly most malicious. Those who believe that it is possible to make peace believe that ethically normative practices designed to alleviate conflict are historically significant and functionally feasible. They resist any policy of closure that gives up on the search for cooperative human interaction. This statement is typical of those who place their trust in this approach:

> We believe the practices of just peacemaking are ethically normative because they bring peace, they solve problems, they promote justice and cooperation in a world whose wars are immeasurably destructive. We see historical evidence that when these normative practices are carried out, they can accomplish the goals of peace and justice.[2]

Although the authors of this statement believe peacemaking has pragmatic consequences, they find the practices they advocate to be based on deeply held faith perspectives that have a more ultimate claim on their lives than any experiential evidence. While the way of describing such faith perspectives may vary from tradition to tradition (even from individual to individual), all those convictions are based on a deep and abiding faith that peace rather than conflict represents God's will for humankind. Discipleship as fidelity to that divine intention is central, but not necessarily always uniform in how it formulates its ideas or expresses this fundamental trust. Just peacemaking practitioners express their commitments to these essential values in a variety of ways.

Central to this position is a concept of justice that directs the fair treatment of all persons, particularly of those who have been marginalized by the social structures of their time.

> The worldwide push and pull for human rights for minorities and oppressed peoples since World War II, since the U.N. [i.e., the Universal] Declaration of Human Rights and the active work of many church groups as well as secular groups, has been a major factor in advancing justice and democracy and is a crucial practice for peacemaking.[3]

The view of human rights espoused by peacemakers differs from an alternative view of human rights that is rooted in eighteenth-century Lockean tradition—an individualistic view of human rights sharply in contrast with the Christian tradition despite its appeal to many religious conservatives. These are two very different views of human rights—one that "emphasizes liberty as autonomy, rejecting monarchy and authoritarianism, and . . . emphasizes the pursuit of property," and the other "that emphasizes community, responsibility, and basic human needs."[4] These two views are not to be confused, and they lead to very different policies. The second of these views of human rights is consistent with peacemaking; the other is an invitation to conflict because it legitimizes the unrestrained pursuit of private gain and often leads to great privilege and enormous inequalities.

Some just peacemakers take the Bible more definitively than others; some accept church traditions as more normative than others; some place more confidence in reason and/or experience than others. Such differences about the nature of theological authority are not merely tolerated, but welcomed as parts of a richer whole. Even when the specific theological elements are not cited, they may well be present in the background. The common factors are important. Those who embrace peacemaking are less preoccupied with eliminating evil than with achieving constructive goods; less with pointing out why others are incorrigible than with exploring how they may be brought into encounters that will make cooperation possible; less with pointing out what cannot be done than with discovering what is worth trying. Although such a perspective sounds idealistic, its advocates regard it as empirically realistic—aware that the continued embrace of conflict in a world in which weapons of mass destruction are possessed by great or lesser powers and can eventually be obtained by persons of ruthless ambition is a dangerous condition. Conflicts are not eliminated merely by decrying their consequences or seeking merely to annihilate certain bad actors, but can be cured only insofar as the dynamics of international behavior are creatively transformed by those who take the risks of trying new initiatives. Moreover, just peacemakers believe that much can be done besides and beyond the official functions of nation-states. Just peacemakers believe they are advocating practices that furnish the basis of a new and creative approach, practices that can be successful. Such approaches

> are empirical practices in our present history that are, in fact, spreading peace. They are engendering positive feedback loops. So they are growing in strength. They are pushing back the frontiers of war and spreading the zones of peace. We believe that because these emerging empirical practices are changing our world for the better and pushing back the frontiers of war, they are moral as well as empirical guides for all responsible and caring persons. They call all persons of good will to lend their shoulders

to the effort. They give realistic guidance for grassroots groups, voluntary associations, and groups in churches, synagogues, meetings, and mosques.[5]

Assumptions behind the Criminal Justice Model

A criminal justice model believes that the restraint of wrong-doing is a unique and professional task to be entrusted to special functionaries whose work is done under careful scrutiny and according to strict standards of responsibility and accountability. It acknowledges the possibility that there will be individuals or groups whose behavior threatens the peace and well-being of the general community, and who do not voluntarily respond to initiatives designed to bring about changes in their behavior. But those who believe in the importance of this model are equally convinced that the behavior of such persons does not call for vindictive or excessive vigilantism that seeks to punish or curtail wrongdoers without due process or that harms innocent bystanders in the process. Those who hold this view understand that efforts to counter malfeasance by the use of coercive means that are not legitimized by a system of justice often lead to consequences (such as lynchings) that are just as threatening to good order as the wrongdoing they seek to eliminate. Summary punishments are not forms of justice but only of vengeance, and while vengeance may assuage anger it does not protect or enrich human well-being or result in good order.

Although the results are far from perfect, the development of law enforcement as a system of justice is one of the important and valuable achievements of societies that surround freedom with constitutional protections. Perhaps the profoundest theological roots for this model are located in the Reformed tradition. The premise on which this model is built is a theologically grounded belief in the role of civil government as the foundation of public order. Calvin put this conviction force-fully: "[N]o one ought to doubt that civil authority is a calling, not only holy and lawful before God, but also the most sacred and by far the most honorable of all callings in the whole life of mortal men."[6] But other religious traditions are also strongly supportive of a law enforcement role for civil government, which some of them believe is founded on the natural law and others understand as ordinances having divine sanction.

Civil government legitimizes efforts, including the re-strained use of force, to curtail wrongdoing within its bor-ders, but self-appointed heroes like Robin Hood and the Lone Ranger do not fit this model. While such figures seek to cur-tail wrongdoing, they do so without the benefits of a struc-ture of justice and order to give such efforts legitimacy and oversee them so as to prevent misuse. Law enforcement is a derivative function, which gains legitimacy from the civil order to which it is responsible. It deals with wrongdoing only within the context of a judicial system. It is subordinate to a judicial system that ensures transgressors will be fairly tried for guilt or innocence before they are punished. John Howard Yoder has astutely noted that police work or law enforcement is morally different from the use of military force. That difference depends upon the extent to which police work is subject to the restraints of civil procedures.

> [T]he state never has a blanket authorization to use violence. The use of force must be limited to the police function, i.e. guided by fair judicial processes, subject to recognized reg-ulations and safeguarded in practice against running away with the situation. Only the absolute minimum of violence is therefore in any way excusable. The state has no general authorization to use the sword independently of its com-mission to hold violence to a minimum.[7]

Those charged with law enforcement bear a very heavy burden. They face danger from those whose behavior they must bring to the bar of justice, and suspicion from many citizens who see "cops" as adversaries rather than protectors of their freedoms. Moreover, the very restrictions on the use of force by law enforcement officers that are so essential to the viability of a free society are not always easy to respect in the harsh and dangerous work of bringing criminals to justice. As crime increases, the police and many members of the public want to remove or lighten such restrictions—to give police stronger tools and greater powers than they have in open societies. But it is those very restrictions that distinguish police work from military action and prevent the exercise of violence from becoming the controlling feature of the social process.

One of the striking things about the field of Christian ethical reflection, at least during the last several decades, is how little attention it has paid to the unique features of law enforcement or the problems that can arise in pursuing it as a vocation. One can go through the indices of book after book in the field and find no entries for either law enforcement or police work. In comparison with the immense amount of thinking about the problem of war and moral issues surrounding military service, this lacuna is telling. In comparison with the page after page and volume after volume dealing with the practice of medicine, the failure to consider the opportunities and the moral difficulties involved in police work may even send a signal that it is not terribly important. Is it any surprise, then, that when a society is faced with a traumatic threat the military model is the only one considered?

In the realm of international affairs as well the policing model has received relatively little consideration because most aggression has normally been done by nation-states rather than by individuals and small groups. The Korean War is sometimes called a "police action" because it involved a deliberately limited strategy to stem an act of aggression by using the military forces of cooperating nations, but it never involved the complex set of functions that are characteristic of the law enforcement model fully understood. International peacekeeping forces have been developed on a military model, not least because threats to peace have been assumed to come from aggression done by nation-states rather than by outlaw groups. Little attention has been given to the alternative patterns of violence being created by the rise of terrorism and why they may pose a problem that should be dealt with in a quite different way. The creation of an international criminal court of justice should be a priority for any international system of law enforcement. The fact that this has not been recognized as such by the United States indicates how far away from adopting the law enforcement model in international relations our country still stands. Those who think that they can be sheriff, judge, and executioner all at once show little understanding of the law enforcement process.

One of the more important differences between a law enforcement model and a military model lies in what each looks for as a possible outcome from its efforts. A system of criminal justice aims to curtail and manage wrongdoing, holding it to tolerable limits. Military action often aims at eliminating wrongdoers, wiping them from the face of the earth rather than limiting or changing their behavior. Law enforcement does not seek "victories" in the same sense as does warfare. It offers the amelioration of problems, not their elimination.

In an observation made many years ago, John Howard Yoder noted that the effort to carry the police function to excess was the source of a great potential evil:

> The danger is seldom that the state authorities will fail to do their job of policing. The universal temptation is rather to overdo this function. Instead of seeing itself as the guardian of the stability of a "tolerable balance of egoisms" within which the work of the church and the socially constructive efforts of men of good will can go forward, the policeman or the statesman comes to consider himself as being responsible for bringing into existence an ideal

order. Since the consequences of fundamental structural changes can never be known, such efforts to organize the ideal society from the top will always be less successful than hoped, but what matters more is that the pretension to be, or to be in the process of becoming the ideal society, is pride, the one sin that most surely leads to a fall, even already within history. Thus the state need not ask to be worshiped to be on its way to becoming demonic; it is sufficient that it place the authority of its police arm behind the pretension to represent that ideal order.[8]

Assumptions behind the Crusade Model

It is precisely the dynamic Yoder describes that leads into the crusade model. This model grows out of a deep conviction that the task of religious people is to challenge and destroy wrongdoing (though seldom ever their own). This task is taken to be a divinely approved (or at least historically destined) duty to play a special role in bringing wrongdoing to an end. In its most morally commendable versions this task is understood as a protection for others rather than merely as a form of self-defense. The depth and the power of this commitment can be very great, prompting heroic resolves and sacrificial efforts. Such resolves are not infrequently cloaked with the mantle of moral self-righteousness. At last—at least in the perception of the crusader—Lord Acton's dictum that power corrupts is proven erroneous, for power is the very thing that enables the crusader to stalk evil, to make the world safe for liberty and liberty free of wrongdoing. This is a theological conviction with great appeal, in which religion provides the moral certainty and the emotive drive to take on very large historical burdens.

Religion is almost always invoked as a support for crusades. That fact is illustrated in many biblical stories, in triumphal actions by the church in much of its history, and in the impact of religious influences on the behavior of many nation-states. A crusade stance involves moral earnestness, not cynicism; self-confident faith, rather than despair. Such a stance creates dedication, reinforces conviction, and overcomes hesitation. Crusades are characterized by attitudes, assumptions, and convictions that give the use of force a special dynamic. Such attitudes can sometimes make even worthy actions into oppressive threats because they are carried out with such intensity. Crusaders feel it is profoundly wrong to sit by and let injustice flourish. For crusaders, religion is an engine of zeal that provides the motivation for acting with unusual resolve and self-confidence. Religion functions this way for a great many people—perhaps for a majority of people—and when it does so it scares many others. It is usually easier to have a dialogue with those whose actions are admittedly pragmatic than with those who believe they are doing God's will.

Crusaders have a clear idea of who the enemy is and why the enemy is evil. Often it is a single person or single group. Seldom do crusaders recognize the complexities of life that often make it difficult to locate the cause of evil with precision, and they are generally unlikely to recognize any way in which their behavior has contributed to the problem. The world is conceived in terms of sharply polarizing contrasts: right versus wrong, innocence versus guilt, malice versus benevolence, faith versus infidelity. Ambiguity, hesitation, complexity, and subtleness are avoided as conceptual plagues—attitudes that undercut the resolves that are considered essential to dealing with evil decisively. The greater the nature of the threat, the more sharply the contrast is drawn. This is both a psychological stance and a theological position. Crusaders tend to regard negotiation or compromise as forms of weakness that only undercut the process of bringing evil to bay. Firmness and resolve are the touchstones of fidelity; rigor, the requisite for success.

Historical Events and Religious Outlooks

Traumatic events not infrequently produce changes in public attitudes, changes that involve major shifts in social outlooks and moral responses. For instance, in 1940–41 America vacillated between isolationism and interventionism until the attack on Pearl Harbor crystallized public support for entrance into the Second World War. Entrance into that war took the form both of declaring war against the Japanese, who assaulted our naval base in the Pacific, and also the form of declaring war on Germany and Italy in order to support the allied nations of Europe that were defending themselves against the threat of totalitarian regimes.

That shift in the posture of the nation was accompanied by an equally significant shift in a good deal of religious and moral thinking. Because there had been so much doubt about the legitimacy of war in religious thinking at the time, a truly important result was the development of an outlook called "agonized participation"—the use of armed conflict to stem a terrible evil associated with the realization that the use of armed conflict must avoid self-righteousness. Although this outlook was not universally shared, it did make moral thinking about the Second World War much different from the attitude of moral confidence that marked the pursuit of the First World War. Many mainline religious groups understood the moral problems involved in using armed conflict, and engaged in war with a pained reluctance, fully aware of its awful nature. While supporting a determined resolve to defeat the enemy, they warned against demonizing the enemy and emphasized the importance of rehabilitating the defeated nations after the conclusion of the hostilities. They helped the nation to take on a job considered necessary without truculence or self-righteousness.

The nearly simultaneous attacks on the World Trade Center and the Pentagon have been traumatic events that have resulted in an equally major change in thinking. This time the debate has not been about whether or not the United States should be involved in world affairs—a matter already rendered moot because in September 2001 the United States had military forces on almost every continent engaged in treaty enforcement, peacekeeping, and even humanitarian intervention. Before those symbols of American power were attacked, much serious consideration was being given to how a strong and powerful nation can use its extensive military capabilities without misusing that power, and what the appropriate limits to that power are.

Just war teaching had become thoroughly elaborated as a part of the public debate, both as a basic way for judging whether a particular conflict is wrong and as a way for contending that a particular conflict is right. The debate has not been whether war as such is right or wrong (the issue between pacifists and nonpacifists as it occurred in an earlier time and still existed in certain circles) but whether or not any particular use of armed conflict can be legitimate. Differences of judgment were particularly strong in the case of Vietnam, but were not absent from the discussion of subsequent conflicts such as the Gulf War.

The attack on the World Trade Center was especially traumatic because it was directed against a civilian place of business rather than against a military installation. Even the attack on the Pentagon affected civilians and military personnel not on guard against hostile actions. These events were unimaginable before they happened and deadly beyond all conceivable expectations. The experience of being attacked so dramatically provided the basis on which the Bush administration understood and defended its response to this trauma. The attacks on the World Trade Center and Pentagon did much to jettison just war thinking and to bring about a resurgence of crusade morality. The rhetoric used by the administration following these attacks reflected a quite different moral stance than that which created the approach of agonized participation following the attack on Pearl Harbor or even the use of military action for limited or humanitarian purposes as in Korea, Vietnam, and the Balkans. The new stance has been marked by rhetoric that draws a sharp contrast between the forces of good and the forces of evil in the world. The term "crusade" was actually used early on, but was subsequently downplayed because it conjures up unfortunate images from the past of Westerners' behavior toward the people of the Middle East. But the moral assumptions have remained those of the crusade even though the term has been bracketed out.

Several consequences have flowed from the use of this basic model. A decision was made to extend the use of military power to enforce the disarmament of Iraq (also to destroy its leader). Although Iraq's defiance of the mandates of the United Nations Security Council had gone on for years preceding the attack on the World Trade Center, after that attack that defiance was considered so dangerous as to require military action to stop it. The crusade against terrorism was applied to a particular nation-state against which there were other grievances. Of course, Iraq could supply terrorists with weapons of mass destruction and offered no assurance it would not do so, but the problem was no greater after the World Trade Center than before. What changed was the sense of urgency thought necessary to deal with the behavior of a particular regime and the possibility that the administration came to regard stern action as a way to bolster its standing with a public whose majority may have been all too ready to see actions taken to deal decisively with troublemakers.

Moreover, a major shift in thinking was made by the administration for guiding defense policy. The idea of deterrence was repudiated and replaced with the idea of the preemptive strike. The idea of cooperative membership in the community of nations was compromised by the embrace of the idea of full spectrum dominance—the idea that America's military power must be overpowering in every part of the world. Although this shift has not been without its critics, it clearly illustrates how deeply the model of the crusade has taken over as the controlling paradigm since the attacks on the World Trade Center and the Pentagon.

Crusade thinking assumes there is an inescapable difference between the civil order within sovereign states and the relationships between them. Relationships between nations are ultimately based on power, not order. Only from such an assumption does the idea of preemption make sense. In closer relationships, for instance, the law acknowledges the legitimacy of self-defense but does not condone preemptive strikes. If a person strikes back when actually threatened with harm, that person's response may be considered prudent and legally permissible. But the threat must be very obvious and clearly imminent. A person who took that initiative and attacked someone merely thought to be a threat, or someone who had expressed hatred and anger but not taken any overt action, would be guilty of assault. The allegation of presumption would not suffice as a defense. The common law does not require turning the other cheek, but it does rule out taking initiatives in starting violence. To adopt the idea of the preemptive strike as legitimate for dealing with large groups is to repudiate the idea that relationships between such groups can ever be marked by the same civility that is so essential in relationships between individuals and smaller groups.

It may not be possible to explain conclusively why the crusade mentality developed so abruptly after September 2001, but it is worth some conjectures. One explanation may stem from the new position that the United States had come to occupy in the world. A crusading stance is a temptation for the powerful, for those who are in a position to exercise power without the threat of counteraction. Crusade thinking is not merely political realism in the sense of calculating how power should be used. It is a form of moral earnestness, motivated by the belief that duty requires the exercise of power to subdue evildoers. It is a version of moral dedication that functions for those who embrace it as a pattern for living, a zeal for doing, and confidence for hoping that this is a divinely mandated destiny. It is a temptation for the strong and powerful.

Another explanation may lie in the type of religion embraced by President Bush. That religious outlook has been astutely described as follows:

> George W. Bush's faith offers no speed bumps on the road to Baghdad; it does not give him pause or force him to reflect. It is a source of comfort and strength but not of wisdom.
>
> The American tradition of wartime leadership seems more subdued. The most memorable images are gaunt and painful: the haunted Lincoln; the dark circles under Franklin Roosevelt's eyes; Kennedy standing alone in shadows during the Cuban missile crisis. This is a moment far more ambiguous that any of those; intellectual anguish is permissible. War may be the correct choice, but it can't be an easy one. The world might have more confidence in the judgment of this President if he weren't always bathed in the blinding glare of his own certainty.[9]

It may be that Bush's stance has been brought about by the role now played by the religious right in American political life. Although conservative theologies can be embraced with modesty, they are not infrequently associated with a moral truculence of the type characteristic of crusade thinking. Those who feel that certainty is the hallmark of proper beliefs are often also convinced that uprightness is the mark of moral correctness. They see tolerance and hesitation as marks of weakness in front of evil. Such religious conservatism was not politically active in the 1940s because then most Christian conservatives deemed religion to be a private matter and efforts to control public life to be outside the sphere of religious duty.

That has changed, and that change may also help explain why the crusade model has now become so influential.

Yet another explanation for why the attacks of September 11 resulted in the resurgence of a crusade response builds on observations that have been developed by the journalist Chris Hedges. According to Hedges, war provides a special sense of purpose and meaning that is often missing in ordinary experience:

> The enduring attraction of war is this: Even with its destruction and carnage, it can give us what we long for in life. It can give us purpose, meaning, a reason for living. Only when we are in the midst of conflict does the shallowness and vapidness of much of our lives become apparent. Trivia dominates our conversations and increasingly our airwaves. And war is an enticing elixir. It gives resolve, a cause. It allows us to be noble.[10]

The conflicts in which the United States has been engaged ever since the Korean War have not produced the consequences to which Hedges points. They have been accompanied by endless debates—serious and important debates about their legitimacy—but debates that have not been resolved. There has been disillusionment with the consequences of military engagements that have had only modest success. The debates have taken away the thrill of patriotism and the sense of meaning that brings out a version of nobility. Partial success has been the best of the outcomes, if indeed even that. The terrorist attacks were so outrageous as to dispel the pale of uncertainty that marked the atmosphere surrounding many of the more recent conflicts. That could make a sense of national purpose respectable, appealing, and worthy of unrestrained embrace.

> Nationalist triumphalism was shunned and discredited in America after Vietnam. We were forced to see ourselves as others saw us, and it was not always pleasant. We under-

stood, at least for the moment, the lie. But the plague of nationalism was resurrected during the Reagan years. It became ascendent with the Persian Gulf War, when we embraced the mythic and unachievable goal of a "New World Order." The infection of nationalism now lies unchecked and blindly accepted in the march we make as a nation towards another war, one as ill conceived as the war we lost in southeast Asia.[11]

It is not clear at the time this is written that the military action in Iraq has had the consequences that Hedges anticipated. The enthusiasm that attended what seemed to be initial successes has been tempered as the complexities of the political situation have become apparent. The result may not be a resurgence of nationalistic triumphalism; the cost of bringing a viable political outcome in the aftermath of the military action will sober even the most adamant supporters and may even drive them to seek the support and cooperation of other nations. Moreover, the consequences of this action for subduing terrorism are by no means reassuring. The need to deal with the deeper and more fundamental issues of how the world can become a functioning community of differences that is significantly relieved of the threats of violence will still have to be addressed. How this is carried out may well be the crucial factor in determining the future of peace in the Middle East and the extent to which terrorism persists in the months and years ahead.

Chapter 6

Being Faithful amid Risk, Differences, and Uncertainty

*T*his chapter explores how it is possible to be faithful to several fundamental Christian commitments in the face of the threat that terrorism poses. Terrorism confronts us with challenges that raise issues concerning convictions at the deepest level. But it also highlights the fact that we live in a world that does not have a common mind about such convictions, in which foundational beliefs and moral outlooks are often matters of contention rather than instruments of unity. This means that terrorism must be confronted without the focus provided by a set of common beliefs that bring people together. The threat that terrorism poses will not produce unity where it does not exist nor result in agreements that are otherwise lacking. Terrorism will have to be confronted in a world in which controlling belief systems differ radically, not only between different cultures of the world but even between different moral perspectives within any one tradition.

To realize that this is the case is bound to be disturbing. It may come as a shock to those who believe that freely conducted rational inquiry and open dialogue can lead to agreements around which it is possible to rally. It may be an even greater shock to those who think that religion can offer divinely authenticated guidance that provides the assurance that certain actions are in accord with the will of God. Terrorism is not merely a form of evil behavior with which small groups of malicious actors assault a world that is cohered by a significant set of common values. It is a manifestation—perhaps the most blatant manifestation—of the fact that people differ sharply about what is supremely important.

This does not mean that we can do nothing to alleviate the threat that terrorism poses, but it does preclude the possibility of dealing with terrorism in ways that have unanimous support and are decisively effective. Terrorism will not be stamped out by the mere escalation of resolve, however vehement or single-minded. Differences abound with respect to how terrorism should or can be dealt with. Such differences occur even among adherents of the same religious tradition, and they reflect deep contrasts in foundational assumptions about the nature and the possibilities of the human enterprise.

Neither faith in God nor allegiance to a particular form of government eliminates such differences entirely. Efforts to see that they do so can be counterproductive of the very ends they seek. Religion becomes a form of tyranny whenever it insists that people agree to beliefs and practices they do not accept in their hearts. Democracies cannot be satisfactorily maintained by forcing people to abide by policies they do not accept. Coercion can create behavioral conformity, but it cannot bring about the embrace of loyalties that make for true and viable community.

To be faithful in the face of terrorism does not consist of having a strategic blueprint for particular actions. Rather it means embracing a perspective in which patience and confidence enable differences to be reconciled into a diverse whole. While this precludes giving a single strategy total dominance, it does not preclude taking actions that seek to alleviate antagonisms. While this precludes seeking a total destruction of evildoers, it does not preclude trying to hold evildoing at bay and to minimize its consequences. While this precludes assuming that the world must be clobbered into conformity, it does not preclude seeking to unite diverse efforts to improve the human condition.

The danger terrorism poses may be less in what it can do to harm us than in what it prompts us to do to harm ourselves. If we lose confidence in our own best inclinations, thinking that threats can only be dealt with by mounting counterthreats, that deceit can only be met by clandestine cleverness, surprise only offset by countersurprise, and violence stemmed only by counterviolence, terrorism will have reshaped us even if we think we have overcome it. If we curtail freedoms in the process of defending freedom, what is the benefit? We need a positive resurgence of our noble convictions rather than the embrace of strategies that merely mirror the stances of those we seek to oppose. Such a response to terrorism is possible only in the context of a very vital practice of a faith deeply rooted in compassion.

Living with Risk

In thinking about the way or ways religious faith can help to shape responses to terrorism, there may be no more important starting point than to deal with the experience of vulnerability. Vulnerability is not some new reality that suddenly sprang forth in September 2001. It is a basic feature of human existence. Everyone is vulnerable in a variety of ways. We accept risks in order to live. We place ourselves at risk whenever we drive an automobile, fly in an airplane, expose ourselves to infections when shopping in a mall or attending church. Life cannot be lived without accepting risks, many of which are statistically far more threatening than the prospects of being a victim of a terrorist attack.

Although efforts to minimize risks are important and should be pursued as prudently as possible, without risks there can be no active living. How then do we decide which risks to take as a matter of normal living and which risks have to be curtailed as quickly and as fully as possible? Why do some risks seem acceptable while other risks are considered intolerable and must be eliminated at very great cost? Differences in attitudes toward risk taking reveal much about the value commitments of various groups. Consider, for instance, how environmental risks are seemingly taken lightly by some of the very same people who find the risks posed by terrorism to be completely unacceptable. In facing the first, economic concerns are apparently controlling; in dealing with the second, they seem to be easily discounted. Why is it possible to persuade people to take risks by engaging in conflicts for the purpose of destroying others but not to take risks in order to avoid becoming agents of destruction?

Terrorism poses risks. It will probably do so no matter how much we seek to curtail it. To suppose that we can be made entirely safe from the threat that terrorism poses is to yearn for the impossible, yet much counterterrorist rhetoric seems to seek just that consequence. Such yearnings can be dangerous because they lead to false expectations or else prompt actions that become excessive and may even take place in desperation. For instance, an effort to eliminate risk may prompt a nation to curtail freedom to the point where open social interchanges are threatened or reduced so much as to change the quality of public life in a free society. We must realize that this consequence has considerable attraction, especially when public officials are expected to keep people safe. But to limit freedom in order to achieve total security is to destroy the most valuable and satisfying features of open societies. Although the possibility this will happen as a result of responding to terrorism might seem to be remote, the lessons of history show it cannot be discounted. Dictatorships often arise from the efforts of rulers to avoid risk by completely controlling all subordinate decision making, and such efforts are often accepted by people who see them as the only way they can be protected from threats. Threats are frequently just as dangerous for the measures people take to eliminate them as for the damages they may directly cause.

The other consequence of seeking to be overly secure is to employ excessive violence against those who are judged to be threats. It is one thing to deter threats; another to seek the elimination of all danger. Terrorism by its very nature will never be entirely destroyed. It can be mounted with little prior warning on such a small scale that there will always be persons tempted to employ it. No reasonable (and probably not even unreasonable) levels of restraint can assure it will not be practiced somewhere, sometime, and by somebody. We have to live with this prospect—doing what can be done to reduce its probability, but avoiding the illusion it can be destroyed completely and avoiding the excesses that are likely to result if that illusion is the driving impulse behind policy making.

Dealing with risk is a decision of faith—not the kind of faith that promises security or offers a false peace, but faith that life can be lived in the prospect that it may well be accompanied by adversity. Such faith stems from reliance upon a God whose purpose has never been to render history harmless, but to offer the resources to cope with circumstances that are never ideal. In contrast to the use of religion by terrorists to bolster destructive zeal, it is possible to embrace religion as a source of prudent confidence and a resolve to live with the risks that attend all human well-being. Doing so permits the pursuit and benefits of other values. Rather than to let fear destroy the very dynamics that make living worthwhile even though marked by uncertainty, faith should guard against all efforts to impair human activity in order to make it completely safe.

None of this furnishes a blueprint for specific actions, but it does furnish a frame of mind that can help to guard against taking actions that are self-defeating. It provides a check on strategic excesses that try to do too much. Taking horrendous measures in order to eliminate risks from human life has the potential for making responses to terrorism destructive of many of the most cherished values that free persons should preserve. Utopian agendas often lead to demonic excesses. To be faithful is to struggle to see that does not happen.

Accepting Diversity

For some time the world has been undergoing a process often referred to as "globalization." This is a complex set of changes that are making all groups more interdependent, economic processes more international and even transnational, and cultural interactions more inevitable. It is increasingly apparent that our world is made up of a vast variety of communities and institutions. Peoples of which we would not have been aware even a few decades ago are now realized to be neighbors whose behavior affects our lives for good or ill. Moreover, there has been an enormous expansion of diversity in our own society. It is no longer possible nor appropriate to think of the United States as a Christian nation, not even as a Judeo-Christian nation. Moral practices have undergone striking transformations and are still in the process of being altered and multiplied in ways that are not always reassuring to those who feel that agreement is necessary for unity. There is no longer comfort to be had in ethnic similarity, nor security in conformity to a single religious or moral outlook. Those bases for social interaction have been dealt a lethal blow, though that does not prevent many people from yearning for their return. Covenant as a function of conformity is no longer possible. Too much has been shaken up.

This process has been going on quite apart from the advent of terrorism, though curiously it may be one of the factors that impels the rise of terrorism. To the extent that terrorism expresses dismay over the development of a diverse and complex world, and stems from a religious perspective that seeks to reestablish a simplistic unity of commitment and purpose, terrorism bears a close kinship to the effort of the Christian right in our own country to see that convictional and moral unity is regained. Any thrust to regain or assert such convictional or moral unity on the part of one group in the world will crash against a similar thrust of other groups to do the same from different convictions. When this happens there is no escaping conflict. Belief becomes the occasion for demanding that others convert to our way of thinking or be destroyed. Preaching becomes less an invitation to a faithful response to the truth that should claim us and more a way of asserting a truth that we must use to override others.

The contrast between these two postures is found in almost every religion. Almost every religion has those who feel that doctrinal uniformity and behavioral conformity are the hallmarks of fidelity. Adherents of this posture may even constitute a majority in each tradition, or at least its militant and possibly most active cadre. This stance is not an instance of bad faith in the sense of being insincere, but its practice is increasingly problematic precisely because the world is becoming a geographical and economic whole without becoming a more single-minded neighborhood. To seek uniformity as a source of unity and security prompts the illegitimate characterization of alternative convictions as forms of infidelity and even leads true believers to think they are doing God's will by ridding the world of those who do not conform to proper orthodoxies and proper orthopractices. Strangely enough, such impulses for conformity motivate both terrorists and strident forms of counterterrorism. Such behavior has appeared in isolated instances in which Christian clergy have attacked Islam as inferior or as perverse.[1] Such ideological intolerance has not been manifested by the Bush administration; indeed, it has generally repudiated such a stance in its claim that American policy is not aimed against the humane forms of Muslim faith. Even so, many serious and well-informed observers feel that taking unilateral military action against nations in the Middle East will fuel the sense that two religions and two cultures are at loggerheads with each other.

To accept diversity is not a wishy-washy way of saying that convictions do not matter. Rather, it is a theologically grounded way of attesting to a profound realization that no human formulations of truth and no cultural practices have a monopoly on legitimacy. It also requires the grace to accept the views of others as authentic forms of fidelity, and even to be tolerant of ways of living that differ from our own. The rub comes when dealing with those who are not similarly committed to the acceptance of diversity. But it would only be self-contradictory for those who accept diversity to feel they must take out by coercion those who do not agree with them (whether by use of law or by use of weapons). Sometimes the appeal of conformity seems to have an apparent advantage in that it offers a basis on which to act with fervor and dispatch. That appeal is especially attractive to persons for whom living with diversity is uncomfortable.

To live with diversity is to place confidence in God rather than in the completeness by which any human schema, including our own, is totally correct. It is to trust that people can be transformed by a change of the spirit—a change that not infrequently occurs when persons who harbor stances of exclusion come face to face with those with whom they disagree and find they are accepted and respected. That is the kind of transformation that made Paul such a great apostle. His conversion consisted of a repudiation of the demand for conformity and the embrace of a new perspective. Without that great openness he would not have taken a religious perspective born in one cultural tradition and made it significant for another.

Individual faith stances need not be couched in pluralistic terminology providing they do not demand conformity. Every person should be free to give expression to the ultimacy of the faith that provides life meaning, an ultimacy that may be couched in fervent witness to deeply meaningful convictions. But God alone, not any person acting as a surrogate for God, knows the hearts and souls of believers. If God does not zap those whose views are incorrect, who are his followers to think it is up to them to do so?

Tolerating Differences about Participation in War

Questions about whether or not to support the use of military action create some of the greatest tensions a society can experience. Such questions pose the problem of living with diversity in its most acute form. In times of war, criticism of policy is likely to be considered a form of disloyalty; being a dissenter is likely to be confused with being a traitor. It is assumed that everyone will "rally around the flag" when hostilities break out. Indeed, disagreement about policies is frequently considered unacceptable even before that happens. But since participation in war requires actions that create the most difficult and upsetting dilemmas for conscience, the moral problems cannot be escaped by appealing to patriotic conformity without doing violence to the moral convictions of many sensitive and dedicated persons.

The feeling that war should bracket out disagreements is often generated by a crusade. Most religious groups strongly supported America's part in the First World War. Their support of the nation's efforts is described in the book *Preachers Present Arms.*[2] In the United States conscientious objection was considered legitimate only for members of so-called peace churches. Conscientious objection by others was met with public hostility and not infrequently criminal persecution.[3] In the Second World War conscientious objection came to be viewed as a legitimate stance for individual members of mainline churches as well as for members of so-called peace churches, and the various denominations generally supported the claims of those who embraced such a position. However, the law required conscientious objection to be based on opposition to participating in all wars, meaning that those who considered a particular conflict to be wrong had no standing. Pacifist convictions were honored but not just war teaching.

The conflicts since the Second World War, particularly the Vietnam War, have seen a change in public responses to conflicts. Wars have become matters of contention, with people of equally serious moral commitments coming to different conclusions about the legitimacy of using violence to deal with this or that international problem. Debates between the alternatives have not been officially stifled, though public sentiment is not always as protective of differences as are constitutional safeguards of free expression. Moreover, the possibility of conscientious objection to particular wars has never been recognized by the law even though it has been supported in principle by several religious bodies. In short, as we enter an era for dealing with terrorism, and especially as we make war a part of that agenda, there is a deep and unresolved tension in American society about whether or not differences of moral judgment about particular conflicts should be respected. Prowar and antiwar advocates sometimes clash in controversies that can be full of acrimony. For many persons, loyalty to nation is the foundation of citizenship and means accepting whatever policy is the basis of the nation's agenda; for others, loyalty to a transcending moral mandate is controlling, even if that involves challenging the nation's actions. If those who put loyalty to nation first deny the right of others to follow their moral insights, the result is oppression—either official or unofficial as the case may be. Turmoil is bound to follow, especially if neither side is open to the possibility the other side might have a legitimate position.

It is very likely that as we deal with terrorism these disagreements about what are wise and morally legitimate policies will continue, perhaps even grow more intense. The action of the Bush administration in dealing with Iraq by military invasion has been sharply and explicitly criticized by a large and sober group of religious leaders. In contrast to what happened in the case of Vietnam this opposition was expressed even before the advent of the military operations, although it was largely ignored. The fundamental moral difference will not evaporate, even in the face of quick and effective military operations. The discussions about these disagreements are intense, and would become far more intense and divisive were similar actions to be proposed for making a preemptive strike against another country. As military measures become matters of political strategy rather than of imminent self-defense, the right of conscientious objection should be extended to cover moral scruples against particular wars and should be available to members of the armed services as well as to potential conscripts if a draft is reactivated.

But mere opposition is not sufficient. That lets the agenda be set by one side and merely responded to by the opponents. While there is some value in saying no to what is wrong, there is greater promise in creating conditions in which others can say yes to what is right. The more compelling challenge is to propose new and better alternatives for dealing with terrorism, to resist polarizing dichotomies between good and evil that separate the world into opposing camps, and to emphasize that no ways of dealing with terrorism should ever preclude the possibility that nations or groups whose present behavior seems a threat can or will change their ways in order to become helpful and cooperative members of a world community. The United States has not even begun to enlist the cooperative imagination of the many nations of the world in a joint effort to deal with the threat of terrorism in that way. It has even resisted such efforts. Doing this is not an easy task, and it cannot be successful without granting the legitimacy of differences. But until and unless the world community assumes this burden as a constructive and challenging undertaking America's role as a strong and dominant power will only be resented, no matter how much the nation believes it is acting for the benefit of others.

The Place for Forgiveness and Reconciliation

In a book of pivotal insight and powerful suggestiveness, Donald W. Shriver Jr. has focused attention on the role that forgiveness can play in political affairs. Although written before September 11, the argument has acquired added relevance in light of that episode. According to Shriver, the significance of forgiveness for political life has been seriously overlooked by most political philosophy (and, one might add, by a large portion of Christian theology). Shriver explains,

> Forgiveness in a political context . . . is an act that joins moral truth, forbearance, empathy, and commitment to repair a fractured human relation. Such a combination calls for a collective turning from the past that neither ignores past evil nor excuses it, that neither overlooks justice nor reduces justice to revenge, that insists on the humanity of enemies even in their commission of dehumanizing deeds, and that values the justice that restores political community above the justice that destroys it.
>
> So defined, political forgiveness links realism to hope. It aims at delivering the human future from repetitions of the atrocities of the past. Given the scale of politically engineered atrocity in the twentieth century, nothing could be a more practical or more urgent gift to our neighbors of the twenty-first.[4]

Interest in and writing about the significance of forgiveness and reconciliation in political life is developing at a significant rate. For instance, the John Templeton Foundation sponsored a conference on this topic in 1999, and the proceedings were published in a book entitled *Forgiveness and Reconciliation: Religion, Public Policy, and Conflict Resolution*.[5] In the first chapter of this book, editor Rodney L. Petersen writes:

> Forgiveness certainly takes place outside of Christian circles. Some will even contend that—given a track record that includes crusades, inquisitions, pogroms, and the pettiness of everyday church life—forgiveness is better understood elsewhere than in the church. Indeed, this chapter began with such parallel or suggestive terminology as *mercy, compassion,* and *acceptance.* That forgiveness is recognized, given, and received by all people is an aspect of our common identity.[6]

When the World Trade Center and the Pentagon were attacked, nothing could have been further from the public mind than to forgive the action and confound the terrorists by so doing. Such a response might have done much to create the image of a United States totally different from what the terrorists contend it to be. The empathy of other nations that originally recognized the horror of those attacks and treated the United States as a victim deserving of sympathetic support might have continued. By reacting as the United States did, it has lost much of that of support and even come to be viewed with increasing suspicion and concern, not merely by her enemies but by some of her friends. What the truculent would regard as wimpish might have been a source of strength.

A quiet tenacity in the face of evil—a tenacity that seeks the rehabilitation of the wrongdoer—may have far more capacity to change the world than the wielding of the sword. This is not a popular tenet, and to suggest the possibilities that can result from dealing with evil in this way is likely to invite ridicule. Perhaps it is unpopular because it entails accepting the costs of reconciliation on the self rather than imposing them on others. But this is the paradigm according to which God deals with the world. Does this make God weak? To be sure, the cross does not furnish a success story in the ordinary meaning of the term. But what is the basis for holding that the alternative has resulted in success? In a world where violence is escalating and making ever greater numbers of people and ever larger groups more and more vulnerable to ever more horrendous possibilities of injury, what indeed is the warrant for deeming the use of violence a success story? It is highly probable that violence may be on the way to doing in the human race, not providing healing order. To seek the reversal of this scenario would not be a weakness, but a strength. That strength can only stem from an understanding of religion that is wiser than the realism of this world and braver than the heroism of the truculent.

Power as Servanthood

The events of the present time highlight the enigmatic nature of power with ironic intensity. The terrorist attacks on the United States came not in a moment of weakness, but at the point at which its power in the world was unparalleled in scope and strength. It has long been a premise of political realism that to be weak is to invite aggression; hence, power must be maintained as a means of deterring those who would inflict harm on us or on those whom we are responsible to protect. But terrorism mocks the logic which holds that strength is the sole means of providing security. Terrorists are not powerful according to the normal measures of military might. They are not capable of making others do their will because they have massive armaments, but they create consternation

with the intensity of their resolve, their willingness to sacrifice themselves for a cause, and a calculating shrewdness that
seems to acknowledge no limitations on the use of demonic
cleverness. In short, they confound the basic premises on
which all balance-of-power thinking rests.

If this is the case, what are we to say about the way in
which the terrorist attacks have been used to legitimize a new
kind of thinking about the use of power? That new thinking
comes about from the response to the terrorist attacks of September 11, 2001, which have occasioned not merely a resolve
to deal with the specific kind of dangers posed by destructive
and hostile actions, but a major shift in American policy with
respect to the use of military might. Those who have been
making policy since that attack have escalated the response
to terrorism into the occasion for dealing more aggressively
with a number of different threats that have been present in
the world for quite some time. Although the military response
to terrorism began by targeting the Taliban regime in Afghanistan (now despised by Western powers despite their role in
its creation), this thinking soon led to the proposal to attack
Iraq, whose dictatorial leader had defied the will of the
United Nations Security Council mandating disarmament.
The behavior of Iraq hardly deserves approval, but its
malfeasance did not start with the terrorist attacks on the
United States and may have had little or no connection with
those attacks. Saddam Hussein's behavior posed a potential
long-range danger rather than an actual violation of another
nation's territory (which made the situation in 2003 different
from what it was in the Gulf War). The decision to take out
the regime in Iraq therefore represented a decision to use military force as an instrument of policy rather than as a direct
response to an overt act of aggression. This was a decision to
use force for policy reasons, not for defense in the normal
meaning of that term. The drive to attack Iraq was based on
a view of America's role in the world advocated by a group

of thinkers who have gained administrative support for the view that it is the destiny of the now preeminent power in the world to use military and economic power to establish democracy and freedom throughout the globe. While dealing with Iraq's behavior may have been related to countering terrorist activity (the extent to which this is the case has been a matter of debate), the military action against Iraq was an outgrowth of a whole range of reasons that go far beyond the task of dealing with terrorism.

The origins and momentous implications of this new thinking have been described perceptively by Gary Dorrien as evidence of a "unipolarist" agenda.[7] This agenda is no less ambitious than to remake the world according to the idea (its advocates would probably prefer to say ideals) of Western democracy and free enterprise. Although intentioned as benevolent, this agenda has all the functional features of imperial domination. Unlike traditional realism it involves the use of power for dominion and control, not for defense. According to Dorrien,

> a true realism would distinguish between international police action to curb terrorism and wars of aggression against governments and their civilian populations. Realism tells us that there will always be bad leaders who have to be coped with and contained. But a war fought for the reasons that are being given leads inevitably and necessarily to more wars, exactly as its unipolarist advocates insist. We cannot diminish terrorism by incinerating Muslim nations and causing most of the world to despise the U.S.[8]

This unipolarism has not ignored the United Nations, but it has approached the United Nations mainly (perhaps even merely) for confirmation and collaboration of its own agenda, setting forth demands for approval of its agenda that are tantamount to this threat: Approve our actions or else we will go it alone. If the international community backs the agenda of the unipolarist, so much the better—the dominion will be less offensive, less likely to be criticized. But, according to the unipolarist, if the international community expresses hesitation or raises doubts about the proposed strategy, that response is not to be taken seriously and certainly will not be considered a signal to abandon the policy. Such is the new face of dominion; the momentous reconfiguration of moral self-assurance.

But it may be that power can be exercised from another stance. American power might be offered to the international community as a resource. Instead of approaching that community with ultimatums, the United States might approach it with offers to help it deal with terrorism as a problem that concerns every nation. Call it servanthood, perhaps, because suggestions for procedures and for the determination of policy would be placed into the hands of others, who would not necessarily reflect what the United States deems the wisest course of action. It would be quite conceivable for the United States to have gone to the United Nations following the attack of September 11 and said, "We are now aware of the vulnerability some of you have been living with for a long time, and to which every one of us is now clearly open. We need an overall plan, devised and supported by the entire international community, for coping with this threat—a threat that up to now has not been faced as squarely as it ought to be. Let us use our corporate wisdom to devise such a plan, which might even look like an international form of policing (appropriately modified). The United States will place its resources at the disposal of the world community as it takes on the challenge of holding terrorism in check."

Something like servanthood may have a possible prototype in the matter of humanitarian intervention, in which American economic and military powers have been used to relieve suffering and even to advance the cause of human rights. Humanitarian intervention is not free of risk nor always successful, but it can involve the use of power within and on behalf of members of a world community. In some respects it is a new use of military power, which has forced a good deal of soul searching as to its moral implications. Traditionalists have been suspicious because it is insufficiently realistic; pacifists because it utilizes military means to accomplish its objectives. Moreover, humanitarian intervention has required rethinking of the just war doctrine of last resort, because there are many reasons why it makes sense to use it as early as possible. It also may involve crossing international boundaries (as does neo-imperialism). But both early intervention and the crossing of international boundaries have very different moral implications when they are forms of servanthood than when they are instruments of domination. Only by recognizing that fundamental difference can America's role escape the moral arrogance that so frequently bedevils empires.

The difference between the stance of dominion and the stance of servanthood is fundamentally a theological difference. One is a form of playing God; the other is an acknowledgment of being human. The temptation to take on the world and make it into the image of our own ideals, especially by the use of power, is a form of idolatry, even in morally plausible versions. Even if not mistaken about how democracy and freedom are achieved (as it may well be), it is mistaken in believing that one nation or group, however well intentioned, can impose virtue on others. Community is possible only between persons of moral modesty, between persons who are able to live with differences, who give a little here and there in order to allow others to live, and whose response comes from their own inclinations and convictions and not from subservience to others. There is a moral difference between resisting those who would take away our rights and the rights of those who depend upon us for sustenance and protection and insisting that everyone else must adopt the strategies we propose. One is a version of self-defense and neighbor protection; the other a form of hegemony.

There is a sense in which the concept of servanthood can convey the wrong impression. Servanthood may connote merely taking orders and doing only what is asked for by others. But the best servants do not sit around doing nothing until they receive instructions. They anticipate needs; they proceed proactively, not merely reactively; they are creatively helpful, not just passively submissive. Each of the models for dealing with terrorism—the preemptive stance of the crusade, law enforcement, and peacemaking—offers the greatest promise only if it is undertaken proactively. The preemptive strike, despite problems it raises, is an effort to deal with a problem by taking the initiative, not just sitting back to await the crisis. Any progress toward achieving a law enforcement model for the international community to cope with terrorism will come about only if strong initiatives are jointly taken by the world community. The peacemaking model has the taking of reconciling initiatives as one of its most crucial features. Servanthood provides a model in which initiatives are possible that make the welfare of the whole world (including our interests) and not merely self-interest the reason for taking action. The gospel is a call to resist the impulse to full spectrum domination and replace it with full spectrum servanthood.

Notes

CHAPTER 1: WHAT IS TERRORISM?

1. Paul R. Pillar, *Terrorism and U.S. Foreign Policy* (Washington, D.C.: Brookings Institution Press, 2001), 12.

2. 22 U.S.C. 2656f (d).

3. See Pillar, *Terrorism and U.S. Foreign Policy,* 12–13, for a fuller discussion of these conditions.

4. See Martha Crenshaw, "The Logic of Terrorism: Terrorist Behavior as a Product of Strategic Choice," in *Origins of Terrorism: Psychologies, Ideologies, Theologies, States of Mind,* ed. Walter Reich (Washington, D.C.: Woodrow Wilson Center Press, 1998), 7–8.

5. Jerrold M. Post, "Terrorist Psycho-logic: Terrorist Behavior as a Product of Psychological Forces," in Reich, ed., *Origins of Terrorism,* 25. Italics in original. Post does not use the term pathology, which might be considered somewhat pejorative, but I think it is applicable.

6. Crenshaw, "Logic of Terrorism," 19.

7. Ibid., 11.

8. Post, " Terrorist Psycho-logic," 25–26.

9. Ibid., 27.

10. Ibid.

11. Ibid., 36.

12. Ibid., 38, italics in original.

13. Cindy C. Combs, *Terrorism in the Twenty-First Century,* 3d ed. (Upper Saddle River, N.J.: Prentice-Hall, 2003), 29.

14. Susan Neiman, *Evil in Modern Thought: An Alternative History of Philosophy* (Princeton, N.J.: Princeton University Press, 2002), 283.

15. Walter Laqueur, *The New Terrorism: Fanaticism and the Arms of Mass Destruction* (New York: Oxford University Press, 1999), 3–4.

16. See Kenneth Anderson, "Who Owns the Rules of War?" in *New York Times Magazine*, April 13, 2003, 40.

17. Laqueur, *New Terrorism,* 4.

18. Paul Wilkerson, "The Laws of War and Terrorism," in *The Morality of Terrorism: Religious and Secular Justifications,* ed. David C. Rapoport and Yon Alexander (New York: Pergamon Press, 1982), 314.

19. Combs, *Terrorism in the Twenty-First Century,* 25–26.

20. Ibid., 10.

21. Ibid., 10, italics in original.

22. Alan M. Dershowitz, *Why Terrorism Works: Understanding the Threat, Responding to the Challenge* (New Haven, Conn.: Yale University Press, 2002), 4.

CHAPTER 2: THE CAUSES OF TERRORISM

1. Michael Ignatieff, "The Burden," *New York Times Magazine,* January 5, 2003, 24.

2. See Anne L. Barstow and Tom L. Driver, "Opposing the War in Colombia: A Case for Putting Values to Work," *SVHE Today: A Newsletter of the Society for Values in Higher Education* 39, no. 2 (January 2003): 3–4.

3. For example, see the action of the Presbyterian Church (U.S.A.), *General Assembly Minutes 1995,* 93.

4. *"The Pope Speaks: The Church Documents Bimonthly,"* Our Sunday Visitor 48, no. 2 (March/April 2003): 81.

5. For example, the pastors of at least four prominent churches in New York City were pacifists throughout the duration of the war.

6. This phase was used by the *Christian Century* when it announced its shift away from a pacifist/noninvolvement position to one supporting the war effort.

7. I used this term in *War and Conscience in America* (Philadelphia: Westminster Press, 1968), 41–47. Others have used the phrase "conscientious participation."

8. This phrase was taken from the title of a commission appointed by the Federal Council of Churches and headed by John Foster Dulles to study the making of peace following the conclusion of hostilities.

9. See Telford Taylor, *Nuremberg and Vietnam: An American Tragedy* (Chicago: Quadrangle Books, 1970).

10. "Confronting the War in Vietnam," in *Church and Society Background Papers*, adopted by the Counseling Committee on Church and Society, February 27, 1968, 9.

11. National Conference of Catholic Bishops, *The Challenge of Peace: God's Promise and our Response: A Pastoral Letter on War and Peace,* May 3, 1983; and United Methodist Council of Bishops, *In Defense of Creation: The Nuclear Crisis and Just Peace* (Nashville: Graded Press, 1986).

12. The same situation with respect to just war teaching was evidenced in the debates that took place later about the proposal to mount a war against Iraq in 2003. For instance, George Weigel argued that just war thinking led to a strong mandate to pursue that war ("Moral Clarity in a Time of War," *First Things,* January 2003, 20–27); whereas George Hunsinger argued strongly that such a war would be a violation of just war principles ("Iraq: Crisis of Confidence: Guest Viewpoint," *Presbyterian Outlook,* September 23, 2002, 4–6, 25. A shorter version of this position appeared in *Christian Century* 119, no. 17 [August 14–27, 2002]: 10–11).

13. An exception has been the action of the Presbyterian Church (U.S.A.) to think through the implications of the practice. See the "Resolution on Just Peacemaking and the Call for International Intervention for Humanitarian Rescue," adopted by the 210th General Assembly, 1998.

14. See John R. Hall, "Religion and Violence: Social Processes in Comparative Perspective," in *Handbook of the Sociology of Religion,* ed. Michele Dillon (New York: Cambridge University Press, 2003), 359–84.

15. See Mark Juergensmeyer, *Terror in the Mind of God: The Global Rise of Religious Violence,* updated ed. with a new preface (Berkeley, Calif.: University of California Press, 2000).

16. While I am indebted to insights in Juergensmeyer's book, the terminology here is largely my own.

17. Juergensmeyer, *Terror in the Mind of God,* 146.

18. See Lloyd Steffan, *The Demonic Turn: The Power of Religion to Inspire or Restrain Violence* (Cleveland: Pilgrim Press, 2003).

19. Rene Girard, *Violence and the Sacred,* trans. by Patrick Gregory (Baltimore: Johns Hopkins University Press, 1977), 284.

20. Ibid., 306.

21. Ibid., 318.

CHAPTER 3: MODELS FOR COUNTERING TERRORISM

1. Paul R. Pillar, *Terrorism and U.S. Foreign Policy* (Washington, D.C.: Brookings Institution Press, 2001), 5–6.

2. See Pillar, *Terrorism and U.S. Foreign Policy,* chapter 4.

3. White House Office, *The National Security Strategy of the United States of America,* September 2002, http://library.nps.navy.mil/uhtbin/hyperion-image/nss.pdf.

4. Ibid., 6.

5. Pillar, *Terrorism and U.S. Foreign Policy,* 217–18.

6. Glen H. Stassen, *Just Peacemaking: Transforming Initiatives for Justice and Peace* (Louisville, Ky.: Westminster/John Knox Press, 1992), 37–38.

7. Glen Stassen, ed., *Just Peacemaking: Ten Practices for Abolishing War* (Cleveland: Pilgrim Press, 1998).

8. Glen Stassen, "Turning Attention to Just Peacemaking Initiatives That Prevent Terrorism," in *Bulletin of the Council of Societies for the Study of Religion* 31, no. 3 (September 2002): 59.

9. United States Institute for Peace, "Strategic Nonviolent Conflict: Lessons from the Past, Ideas for the Future: A Special Report," May 1, 2002, 1, http://www.usip.org.

CHAPTER 4: TERRORISM AND THE EROSION OF CIVIL AND POLITICAL LIBERTIES

1. Timothy Lynch, "Breaking the Vicious Cycle: Preserving Our Liberties While Fighting Terrorism," *Policy Analysis* 443, June 26, 2002 (Washington: Cato Institute), 1.

2. David Little, "Terrorism, Public Emergency, and International Order: The U.S. Example," 6. The author shared a prepublication draft of this paper with me. It is planned for publication by the Institute of Philosophy and the Study of Religions, University of Denmark, Odense, Denmark and is available at http://www.pcusa.org/acswp/wwd/wwd-violence.htm.

3. Ibid., 8.

4. Ibid., 11; italics in original.

5. Alan M. Dershowitz, *Why Terrorism Works: Understanding the Threat, Responding to the Challenge* (New Haven, Conn.: Yale University Press, 2002), 144.

6. Jane Mayer, "Lost in the Jihad: Annals of Justice: Why Did the Government's Case against John Walker Lindh Collapse?" *New Yorker,* March 10, 2003, 50–59.

CHAPTER 5: RELIGION, MORALITY, AND TERRORISM

1. For helpful overviews of the idea of peacemaking see Ronald H. Stone, *The Ultimate Imperative: An Interpretation of Christian Ethics* (Cleveland: Pilgrim Press, 1999), especially chapter 12. Also see Glen H. Stassen, ed., "Resource Section on Just Peacemaking Theory," *Journal of the Society of Christian Ethics* 23, no. 1 (Spring/Summer 2003): 169–284.

2. Duane K. Friesen, John Lagen, S.J, and Glen Stassen, "Just Peacemaking as a New Ethic," in *Just Peacemaking: Ten Practices for Abolishing War*, ed. Glen Stassen (Cleveland: Pilgrim Press, 1998), 5.

3. Ibid., 13.

4. Ibid.

5. Ibid., 2.

6. John Calvin, *Institutes of the Christian Religion* 4.20 (4); Library of Christian Classics, ed. John T. McNeill, trans. Ford Lewis Battles (Philadelphia: Westminster Press, 1960), 2:1490.

7. John Howard Yoder, *The Christian Witness to the State* (Newton, Kans.: Faith and Life Press, 1977), 36–37.

8. Ibid., 37.

9. Joe Klein, "The Blinding Glare of His Certainty," *Time*, February 23, 2003, 19.

10. Chris Hedges, *War Is a Force That Gives Life Meaning* (New York: Public Affairs Press, 2002), 3.

11. Ibid., 61.

CHAPTER 6: BEING FAITHFUL AMID RISK, DIFFERENCES, AND UNCERTAINTY

1. For a helpful overview of several instances of anti-Islamic rhetoric, see Deborah Caldwell, "How Islam-Bashing Got Cool," *Religious Studies News: AAR Edition* 38, no. 4 (October 2003): 13, 27.

2. Ray Hamiton Abrams, *Preachers Present Arms* (New York: Round Table Press, 1933).

3. See Norman Thomas, *Is Conscience a Crime?* (New York: Vanguard Press, 1927).

4. Donald W. Shriver Jr., *An Ethic for Enemies: Forgiveness in Politics* (New York: Oxford University Press, 1995), 9.

5. Raymond G. Helmick, S.J., and Rodney L. Petersen, eds., *Forgiveness and Reconciliation: Religion, Public Policy, and Conflict Resolution* (Philadelphia: Templeton Foundation Press, 2001).

6. Rodney L. Petersen, "A Theology of Forgiveness," in Helmick and Petersen, eds., *Forgiveness and Reconciliation,* 21.

7. Gary Dorrien, "Axis of One: The 'Unipolarist Agenda,'" *Christian Century* 120, no. 5 (March 8, 2003): 30–35.

8. Ibid., 33.